# Productivity Management

## Keane's Project Management Approach for Systems Development

*Second Edition*

Updated and Revised by
**Donald H. Plummer, PMP**

**KEANE**

Keane, Inc., Boston, Massachusetts

*Library of Congress Cataloging in Publication Data*

Keane, Inc.
    Productivity management, Keane's project management
approach for systems development.

    Includes index.
    1. Industrial productivity—Management—Data
proccessing.   I. Keane, Marilyn.   II. Teagan, Mark.
III. Title.

HD56.K42   1984        658.5'0028'54        84-9955
ISBN 0-13-725383-4 (case)

Fifth Printing, 1995

5   6   7   8   9   10

ISBN 0-13-725383-4 (CASE)

*To the hundreds of technical and management professionals at Keane, Inc., who tirelessly invested of themselves in the relentless pursuit of project acceptance—who achieved lofty goals, but at the same time learned from their successes and their failures—and who had the foresight to share their experiences with us and others.*

To order copies of *Productivity Management, Keane's Project Management Approach for Systems Development*, call 1-800-239-0296.

# Table of Contents

# List of Figures

# List of Exhibits

# Preface

By John F. Keane
President and CEO
Keane, Inc.

This is a book about managing projects. It is not one person's view from academia, but rather an accumulation of knowledge earned the hard way—through real-life experience. Like Keane, Inc. itself, this book has grown and evolved to match the requirements of the increasingly sophisticated and complex environments within today's Information Technology organizations. Yet, despite this evolution, the original concepts of Productivity Management remain as true and as valuable today as when the first edition of this book was created by my wife, Marilyn Keane, Mark Teagan and me in 1984.

Application software is the magic that transforms a piece of generalized hardware into a functioning and valuable tool for conducting business. Whether on mainframes or powerful workstations, much of this software is custom created to handle the unique requirements of a particular business. Building these application software systems requires considerable business knowledge and technical expertise. An even greater challenge is presented by the task of managing the disparate activities that, when properly orchestrated, result in a successful system development effort. The extent of this challenge is indisputable, and the cost of not meeting it, enormous. A survey of MIS executives conducted by the Standish Group found 84% of the surveyed application development projects were either not completed, or experienced significant cost and time overruns, carrying a cost to their organizations of $81 billion in failed projects and $59 billion in cost overruns.

Having delivered tens of thousands of software development projects since 1965, Keane has learned to manage projects within numerous technical and business environments. Our growth and success depend on our ability to deliver these projects on time and on budget. With the dedication of our staff, we accomplished these goals, in part, by understanding the unique characteristics of project management for software development.

Software development projects differ from more traditional projects, such as building a house. Building software requires more than a strong technical staff. Successful projects require the involvement of many other individuals from a variety of corporate business units, individuals who have their own important jobs that demand their time and skills. Further, many of these individuals have little experience with software projects and little understanding of the development process. Also, project managers assigned to guide the project do not have line authority over all of the critical resources needed to successfully deliver the project. Thus, they have responsibility and accountability without authority. As technology advances, these challenges increase. For example, enterprise-level client-server applications significantly broaden the concentric circle of people required for a software development project. Understanding these challenges allows project managers to plan for their resolution.

Keane as an organization did not learn these lessons lightly. When we were founded in 1965, good project management consisted of a project manager's "word," and the intensity of a small team of professionals dedicated to doing whatever was necessary to get the job done on time and within budget. This form of project management worked until, after a vacation in 1971, I returned to find seven projects running over budget. This was a devastating situation for a young and growing company. We could not afford to develop project managers by giving them projects to fail on. An exhaustive analysis "post-mortem" followed to uncover the root causes of these failures. We discovered several issues, such as undefined acceptance criteria and failure to involve the right people at the right time, in common within each of the failed projects. Our focus was not on simply correcting the mistakes, but rather on identifying the practices that would prevent similar problems from happening in the first place. Mistakes will happen; however, the goal is to keep them small, keep them one of a kind and share experiences to save others from making the same mistakes. The six principles of Productivity Management described in this book is an outgrowth of this exercise.

Productivity Management (PM) was originally developed for internal use. We use it as the foundation of all of Keane's software development, maintenance and management methodologies, and our employees are trained in the PM principles to ensure that they are prepared for the challenges that await them. PM has also been taught to thousands of our clients. They use PM to understand why Keane project managers insist on certain steps and activities and, more importantly, as a foundation for their own project management approach. Through this book and through our PM Training seminars, the principles of PM are available to any organization wishing to take advantage of our experience.

PM is not a rigid system of rules and requirements, but rather a set of guidelines and principles that can be adopted to match any of the unforeseen circumstances that invariably arise during software development projects. This book describes the basics of project management, devoting a chapter to each of the six PM principles. The lessons contained within are powerful, yet intentionally simple. They are meant to be easily understood, remembered and applied.

In conclusion, I am pleased to acknowledge the talented group of employees and colleagues who have contributed to the development and revision of PM. First, Marilyn Keane, my spouse and companion, whose immense efforts to understand and structure Keane's project management lessons made the first edition of Productivity Management possible. On this second edition, I want to thank Donald Plummer, who assembled Keane's recent project experiences and shared his own personal knowledge; Bob Atwell and Tom Mechachonis, who served as review committee members; and Bob Wyatt, the book's project leader, whose dedication is noted and appreciated. Also, the teamwork of Larry Vale, Michael Richmond, and Mary Prendergast, on editing and proofreading, and John Davalos, Mim Brooks Fawcett, and Leigh Schofield, on design and illustration, was instrumental in bringing this second edition to its successful publication.

I am proud of Keane's track record in project management and delivery, and I am proud of the dedicated employees who have made this track record possible. This book is offered to you as the embodiment of their collective knowledge. I hope that you, like the pioneers to whom this book is dedicated, will use Productivity Management to chart your own courses, and will share your new gained experiences with those yet to explore the technology challenges ahead.

*John F. Keane*

# Introduction

Computers are the ultimate symbol of efficiency. There seems to exist software to facilitate almost every aspect of life, from running an assembly line to running a dishwasher. Technical advancements over the last several decades have enabled us to process, calculate, monitor, communicate, simulate, forecast, store, compare, organize, and sort and resort with a level of speed and efficiency unimaginable just one generation ago.

Curiously, however, one technical area has not changed: the development of computer systems remains one of the most labor-intensive and difficult-to-manage undertakings in the modern economy. This is just as it was during the development of the first commercial computers nearly fifty years ago. Despite decades of experience, information technology still suffers from an alarming rate of management problems evidenced by huge time and cost overruns, unmet customer expectations, and low employee morale.

Systems development projects have been difficult to control not because of a lack of technical resources, but because of a failure to apply fundamental management concepts. Two reasons for this are (1) since the information systems industry is highly technical and rapidly changing, the emphasis is on technical skills and training at the expense of management training, and (2) most information systems managers have come up through the technical ranks and have had little opportunity to develop management skills.

Information technology is littered with the bleached bones of project management techniques designed specifically for the development of computer systems. Most had only minimal success because they were too complex to be applied in the real world. The assumption has been that management of a technical undertaking requires a technical approach. Productivity Management takes a different stance and emphasizes a managerial approach. As described in this book, the Principles of Productivity Management are simple to implement and effective once in place. Those six principles, which are listed below, will guide the project manager through any systems development project:

## The Six Principles of Productivity Management

1. **Define the Job in Detail.** Determine exactly what work must be done and what products must be delivered. Explicitly evaluate the nontechnical environment and customer expectations, and address all areas in writing.

2. **Get the Right People Involved.** Involve the entire project team, including the customers, throughout the project, especially during planning. Ensure that each member of the project team participates in defining his or her own goals.

3. **Estimate the Time and Costs.** Develop a detailed estimate of each phase of the development process before undertaking that phase. Estimate the components of a job separately to increase accuracy. Do not estimate what you do not know.

4. **Break the Job Down Using the 80-Hour Rule.** Break the job down into "tasks" that require no more than 80 hours to complete. Ensure that each task results in a tangible product. The 80-Hour Rule provides the framework for setting schedules, assigning tasks, identifying problems early, confirming time and cost estimates, and evaluating project progress and individual performance.

5. **Establish a Change Procedure.** Recognize that change is an inherent part of systems development. Establish a formal procedure for dealing with changes and ensure that all parties agree to the procedure in advance.

6. **Agree on Acceptance Criteria.** Determine in advance what will constitute an acceptable system. Obtain written acceptances of products throughout the project so that acceptance is a gradual process, rather than a onetime event at the end.

Productivity Management assumes that the project manager already possesses technological proficiency in information systems and, instead, focuses on managing the environment in which systems are developed. The six principles provide techniques that encourage the customers and other nontechnical individuals to become an integral part of the project team.

During the implementation of the Principles of Productivity Management, one discovers the principles have many intertwining and carefully developed relationships that serve as checks on each other.

Before proceeding to the principles themselves, there are a few concepts that will appear throughout this book that need to be discussed briefly. Since Productivity Management concerns the management of projects and systems, we must first define precisely what we mean when we refer to a *project* or a *system.*

## Projects

It would be inappropriate to attempt to apply project management principles to something that is not a project. For the purposes of discussing Productivity Management, a *project* is defined as a specific activity, with a discrete beginning and end, which produces predetermined results. Every project is different, producing a one-of-a-kind product and requiring unique coordination of resources.

Projects must have beginning and end dates. One cannot apply schedules, resources, and cost controls without time constraints to manage against. Although there are times when the approaching dates seem more like the harbinger of our worst doom, they are in fact the keynote to success. We must learn to view deadlines with optimism; they are the principal opportunity to recognize success on a project.

Projects produce unique, predetermined results. Once the result has been obtained, the project is done. If our project is to develop a computer application that will produce weekly sales and commission statements for our sales force, the project is over when we are producing those reports to everyone's satisfaction.

A project is also defined by the existence of limited resources to be managed during the activity. Resources are generally identified as time, money, people, and equipment. When you have a limited supply of resources, you will need to manage them as effectively as possible.

For the purposes of this book and most software development endeavors, a project also demands that there be someone willing to spend money for it and that a project manager be made responsible for the management of the endeavor.

If an activity has all the above characteristics, we can call it a project and apply the Principles of Productivity Management to it. Realize, of course, that the management of every project poses unique problems not covered in traditional management disciplines. Not only do you have to manage people, you must also manage them to a singular, discrete deliverable within tight constraints of time and money. To make matters worse, you often have to manage people who don't really report to you while confronting technological challenges that change for each project. Still, all projects have common characteristics. Understanding these characteristics and how to manage them in the environment of the specific project can change project management from a "work hard and hope for the best" effort into a rational process with likely success.

## Systems

Related to the development of computer applications, projects are almost always tied into *systems* and *systems development*. Very basically defined, a system is an arrangement of things connected to form a whole. The solar system is an arrangement of stars, planets, and other matter that form what is considered a single entity.

Similarly, within business organizations, there exist systems that perform specific functions and can be identified by those functions: marketing systems, manufacturing systems, or accounting systems, for example. An accounting system might be composed of smaller systems such as the accounts payable system, the general ledger system, and the fixed assets system.

Most projects discussed in this book will involve the creation of new systems or the maintenance of old ones.

# 1

# Principle One:
# Define the
# Job in Detail

*… Before You Start.*

# Define the Job in Detail

The seeds of a project's success or failure are sown at its very beginning. If you're looking for a rose but you plant a turnip, you're going to get a turnip. That may seem obvious, but a lot of project managers are planting turnips and expecting rose gardens; that is, they are starting with a poorly defined idea and are expecting winning results. The optimism is admirable, but a healthy dose of realism is in order. Only if you have a clear idea of *what* you are doing will you have any chance of doing it successfully. Clarity is attained by *defining the job in detail.*

## The Basics of Definition

### Definition: Communication, Understanding, and Structure

In order to define a project in detail, it is first necessary to know what is meant by *definition*. In the world of projects, definition generally describes an *activity* or *intent.* "Here is what currently exists, and here is what I intend to do with it." Definition also refers to a description of an activity or intent which others will understand as you understand it. This is often not as simple as you would expect. Have you ever tried getting or giving directions to someone who does not speak the same language as you? In information technology, we have a native language of our own. (If you don't think so, take a moment to go listen in on a group of your peers talking shop, and put yourself in the position of a noncomputer person. Not only do we program in code, but we speak in code as well.) In order for a definition to be understandable, the language in which it is communicated must be understandable by all who will encounter it.

Language is just one small part of the problem. There's also the issue of cognitive understanding. If we all thought in the same way, understanding would be greatly simplified. Unfortunately—or fortunately—we don't, and for a project manager to assume that everyone sees things in the same way is one of the greatest mistakes he or she could make.

Since the development of software—and even the final product itself—is largely intangible, we must use models to help define in a tangible form. Maximum understandability is achieved by communicating the project definition in a written or illustrated medium. Logical process models, data flow diagrams, process flows, entity relationship diagrams, object relationship models, and flowcharts enable the project manager to define a project and to communicate that definition to the development team. While it is not necessarily the project manager's job to prepare every one of these design documents and models, he or she must be certain—by whatever method—that everyone involved has a mutual understanding of the project definition. Failure to ensure mutual understanding among *all* parties involved will likely cause the project and its manager to be perceived as failures.

Any discussion of definition must also note the relevance of information *structure*. Information is infinitely more understandable if it is presented in a structured form. Structured information begins with small amounts of broad, easily understood concepts and gradually works down to more detailed, complex, and related information. Successful project managers must be continually attuned to this important concept throughout the definition process. Hierarchical information structure is vital to understanding basic information processing technology.

## When Does Project Definition Begin?

It is not uncommon for people to be unsure about just when and where a project officially begins. There is no single, correct answer to this question. At Keane, a project typically begins with the **requirements definition** activity. A *feasibility study* frequently precedes requirements definition but is usually treated as a separate activity. A feasibility study addresses questions of potential profit or gain, resource availability, financial ability, and alternatives. If the decision from the feasibility study is to move ahead with a project, then the project formally begins, and you proceed to defining the project requirements with as much detail as is available.

It is sometimes difficult to know when requirements definition is complete. How much definition is enough? How much is too much? You'll probably find that you never have enough documentation and that you always have too much. There is no correct answer, but it helps to evaluate project definition with the following criteria:

1. The customer should know how to test what they are getting; and

2. The project manager should be able to assign reasonably sized work packages to individuals on the development team.

Note that these criteria do not imply that we forego any technical definition. Greater emphasis is placed, however, on the customer, the extended project team, and the project manager's relationships with them.

## The Definition Process

Project definition is best separated along two basic lines: *environmental* definition and *technical* definition (frequently referred to as the "spirit" of project management [environmental] and the "mechanics" of project management [technical]). The former refers to the environment in which the project will be developed, the latter to how the project will be developed. The boundary between the two sometimes becomes a bit blurred, but substantial bodies of definition fall clearly into one category or the other. Recognizing both sides independently will significantly help improve project management success.

The project manager will want to be intimately attuned to the environmental aspects of a project. Projects almost never fail because of purely technical reasons. Technical errors can usually be corrected. Failure to recognize environmental issues, however, such as who is *really* controlling the purse strings and who has final decision-making authority can have calamitous effects. To establish the environmental definition, the project manager must understand the world in which the project is being developed. That world is different for every project: there are different players, different requirements, different outputs, different organizations, and different expectations. A project manager's success will be greatly enhanced by the extent to which he or she understands the unique world of the project.

## Definition Documents

The best mediums for providing definition—both environmental and technical—are the following three documents:

1. The **statement of work;**

2. The **work breakdown structure** that evolves from a systems development life cycle; and

3. **System test plans.**

### Statement of Work

The environmental definition is one area that is best described within a document called the **statement of work.** The statement of work is probably the most important document to a project. More than any other document, it defines what the goals of the project are and allows the project manager to anticipate and prevent problems. The statement of work affirms that the project manager understands who is really in charge of the effort, who is controlling the purse strings, what is the formal and informal organization within which the project will be developed, who are the "kings and queens" that have interest, and other similar but mainly nontechnical issues. It establishes a firm business relationship between the project manager and both the customer and the extended project team. Certain broad elements of technical definition may also be covered in the statement of work, but it is predominantly a management-level document.

Since the statement of work is not a technical document, it is best expressed in simple business terms and common English (or native language). It should not contain items such as data flow diagrams, entity relationship charts, or detailed notes from interviews with customers while determining requirements. Its purpose is to demonstrate that the project team understands the customer's needs and can describe an effective approach to meeting them.

The statement of work demonstrates in writing

1. That the project manager and extended project team understand the problem, opportunity, or need;

2. That the team can adequately describe an approach to meeting the project's requirements;

3. That they have developed a fair estimate of the time, costs, and schedules; and

4. That they have correctly identified the deliverables for the project.

The objective of a statement of work is to ensure that everyone has the same understanding of and expectations for the project. It puts some scope and boundaries around the project and helps identify the extent of the developer's involvement. It provides an opportunity to address potential problems in advance that might not otherwise be resolved until much later in the project. It helps ensure a high level of confidence with all parties involved that the team understands the main problem and how to solve it. Lastly, the statement of work forces the project manager to get everything down in writing, which helps guarantee a common understanding of and agreement on a mutual commitment.

The format of a statement of work, as outlined in exhibit 1, will remain approximately the same from project to project.

Because projects come in widely varying sizes, the length may vary considerably, but whether it is one page or fifty pages, a statement of work must be prepared for every project.

The question is, "What isn't a project; when wouldn't I need a statement of work?" A Keane policy is that if an activity requires more than a person-month, or about 168 hours of effort (not elapsed time), it will be treated as a project, and a statement of work is required. If less, the manager decides whether a statement of work is necessary based on his or her confidence that the activity can be completed on time and within budget without going through the more formal project management process. (It should be noted that you can bring a large organization to rack and ruin by bungling the small projects as quickly as by mismanaging just a few large ones. Better to prepare too many statements of work than too few.)

---

### Exhibit 1: Recommended Structure for the Statement of Work

The statement of work should include the sections listed below. Note that the contents of the statement of work address all six principles of Productivity Management.

#### Project Request

This section contains any formal request forms and their backup documentation. (Remember we want only management information in the SOW, not technical documentation.) If the request was simply a verbal request, put it in writing yourself based on the discussion with the customer. Be sure to note when and from whom the request came.

#### Background

This section contains a description of the chronology of events leading up to the request for service. It is a statement of the customer's requirements in common business language and should demonstrate a basic understanding of the problem.

#### Scope

The scope of a project is defined as "The area or field within which any activity goes on; range or extent of action, observation,

---

**Exhibit 1 (continued)**

and inquiry." Here, you are trying to identify boundaries for the project to determine its size. In order to define the scope at this early stage, you should consider to what extent the following items should be involved:

- Departments, divisions, or organizations
- Business functional areas
- Databases
- Higher level managers or executives
- Development staff (how many?)
- Customers and users (who are they and how many?)
- Money (return on investment, IRR, savings, etc.: how much?)

Anything you can think of to help define the size of the project should be included in the statement of work. Also note any risks or assumptions here.

## Technical Approach

This section describes how the project will be accomplished technically. It is here that you identify the major tasks and deliverables. Keep in mind that you should use nontechnical language in the statement of work. You need supply only brief descriptions of the tasks and deliverables in this section. Comprehensive technical treatment will occur later.

## Managerial Approach

This section covers how the project will be managed to a successful conclusion.

- What is the makeup of the project team (hierarchical, empowered, etc.)?
- Who is the project manager?
- What is the experience of the project team?
- What training, if any, will team members receive before the project begins?
- What will be the reporting structure and frequency?
- How often will project team meetings occur?
- Will there be separate technical and managerial meetings?
- Will there be any committees involved?

Exhibit 1 (continued)

- Who will arbitrate in the case of conflict?

You want to communicate to the person reading your statement of work that you have an approach for competently managing the project.

## Deliverable Products

This section defines the principal deliverable products that will require review and acceptance by the appropriate customer, client, or manager. These are frequently defined in the work breakdown structure and depend on the particular software development approach and associated automated tools that will be used.

## Responsibilities

In this section, you should outline the responsibilities of each department and of key individuals. Consider the responsibilities of the following resources:

- Customer department
- Higher level management
- IS management
- Project team
- Operations
- Clerical support
- Outside vendors
- IS support
- Other departments

What is expected of the various resources? When will they be required? You may even find it appropriate to identify the number of hours or percentage of time for certain people.

## Project Plan

The level of detail of the project plan will vary depending on how much time you have spent in the planning stage. At the least, there should be a preliminary project plan to serve the following purposes:

- Identify an initial estimate of how many people are required and what their approximate skill levels need to be.

- Show the management structure of the project.
- Give some indication of who will be responsible for what major task by skill level.
- Estimate completion dates and effort hours for major deliverables.
- Indicate customer involvement—what tasks, how much time and when.

This particular area will be discussed with more detail in Chapter 4, "Break the Job Down Using the 80-Hour Rule."

### Time and Cost Estimates

At the preparation of the statement of work, you should provide an estimate of the effort, costs, and time required to complete the project. It is crucial, however, that the project be defined in as much detail as time allows, and that estimates are made for only those defined areas. Don't try to estimate what you don't know. Provide a range of costs for undefined activities, and state assumptions and risks under which these estimates have been made. Avoid premature precision. This subject is covered in detail in Chapter 3, "Estimate the Time and Costs."

### Change of Scope Procedures

This section spells out the procedure for handling changes outside the scope of the project. Although many companies have adopted a standard change procedure, it is beneficial to restate the change of scope procedure in every statement of work. (See Chapter 5, "Establish a Change Procedure," for details.)

### Acceptance Procedures

In this section, you establish the acceptance criteria and procedure for acceptance which you should have agreed to in advance with the appropriate project personnel. (See Chapter Six, "Agree on Acceptance Criteria," for details.)

Each phase of a project is considered a project itself and will therefore get its own statement of work, however brief. Some projects are small enough that they require only a couple of phases. In a project that groups all design activities in a single phase and all programming and testing in a second phase, we would prepare two separate statements of work. Similarities between these two statements of work will exist, but having both will ensure a clear definition of the discrete tasks involved in each phase. This level of definition will avoid misunderstanding and maximize the likelihood of project success.

For very large projects that may last more than a year or so and involve 15 to 20 developers, the preparation of the statement of work may take six to eight weeks and run 30 to 40 pages. At the other extreme, a statement of work for a 200-hour programming module might be done in a day. Keane recently received a document called "Statement of Work" from a very large organization. It was shrink-wrapped, weighed just over 11 pounds, and ran 687 pages. That is excessive and is not our notion of an efficient, well-prepared statement of work.

## Presenting the Statement of Work

The statement of work should be a formal and polished document. It is the first tangible representation of the project manager, the development team, and the work they will do; it should be well written and neatly packaged.

You should have a face-to-face presentation with all significant participants on the project so you get real feedback. Make sure everyone fully understands the concepts of the statement of work. If possible, walk through the document paragraph by paragraph in the presentation. Encourage questions, and answer them all. Emphasize time and cost and any problem areas. Don't gloss over anything, especially the more difficult items.

Statements of work, if written correctly, have a way of becoming very important documents in a project. When newcomers join the project, you can simply hand them a copy of the statement of work, and by reading it, they will gain a thorough understanding of the project's goals and the approach to attaining them. Customers, support managers, and IS personnel will also frequently show the statement of work to their bosses, particularly in response to questions like "What's going on in your department?" In this manner, the statement of work will frequently "bubble up" several levels above the initial recipients, which is all the more reason to write it in common business terms and structure it for easy understanding.

## Technical Definition and the Systems Development Life Cycle

Before we define the work breakdown structure, we must first discuss the systems development life cycle from which the work breakdown structure is derived.

Every organization should have an established procedure to approach the technical aspects of its projects. This procedure is applied to any systems development project and acts as a guide for the team from initial technical definition to final implementation. This guideline to procedures is commonly called the *systems development life cycle* or *SDLC*. The SDLC provides technical definition based on a phased sequential approach; that is to say, a step-by-step breakdown of the project into manageable pieces or "phases." The intent of such project breakdown is to define a logical, sequential group of activities and deliverables that lead you through the project from phase to phase. (Keane's systems development life cycle is called *Frameworks for Software Development*.) On all projects, particularly large ones, making sure that everything is done in the right sequence is crucial. The systems development life cycle serves as a road map for that sequence.

Surprisingly, many organizations do not have established SDLC procedures. These are the organizations that are more likely to have projects that never end, that cost several times more than anticipated, and that fail to meet the customer's needs.

Some projects do exist that are so unique that existing SDLC procedures, activities, and deliverables are not fully appropriate, but such projects are rare. Virtually all projects will fit within the framework of an SDLC if a little thoughtful effort is applied. Breaking a project down into logical, more easily managed pieces consistently produces superior results.

Before work starts on any phase, applying SDLC procedures to that phase provides a guide to help make customers, developers, and the entire project team agree on (1) the objectives of the phase, (2) the tasks that must be completed, and (3) the products that are to be delivered.

The list of objectives, tasks, and products derived from the SDLC is called a *work breakdown structure.* Additional items are included in the work breakdown structure as they are recognized. Applying the systems development life cycle procedures to the whole project ensures the detailed definition of the technical aspects of the project.

Keane's procedures below provide one example of a proven systems development life cycle. It is regarded as a traditional or "waterfall" life cycle. As one phase is completed—and not until then—we proceed to the next. The sequence of the phases is

1. Strategic Information Planning
2. System Concept Formation
3. Business Systems Analysis
4. Technical Design
5. Construction
6. Customer Testing
7. Transition
8. Operations and Maintenance

Below is an example to illustrate how Keane's SDLC procedures are applied to an actual project.

1. **Strategic Information Planning.** (Ensure that any system development meets the overall organizational goals.)

   A large East Coast bakery was considering installing computers in their 450 delivery trucks. Their goal was to increase efficiency in capturing and dispersing sales and production information. This goal conformed to their overall corporate strategy of limiting geographic growth but increasing efficiency and profitability.

2. **System Concept Formation.** (Provide basic cost-benefit analysis to determine feasibility. Should the organization pursue this activity further?)

   A preliminary analysis concluded that this project could contribute an 8% reduction in returned (stale or damaged) goods and a 4% increase in overall revenue. If the computers could be installed, new systems developed, and existing systems modified for no more than $2.7 million, the project would be profitable for the organization to undertake.

3. **Business Systems Analysis.** (Determine the requirements to address the need, problem, or opportunity that has been identified.)

   Interviews with all relevant officers, directors, and managers from the financial, administrative, marketing, and production areas identified the requirements of the proposed project.

4. **Technical Design.** (Develop the specifications that will meet the requirements identified in the Business Systems Analysis.)

   All parties' requirements were translated into specifications that would determine the size and speed of computers required, programming specifications for new and modified systems, data types and storage needed, and communication devices.

5. **Construction.** (Build or buy the products [computer programs, databases, etc.] that will perform the business functions needed.)

Based on the Technical Design phase, computers, printers, and communication devices were selected and bought, and systems and programs were modified or newly written.

6. **Customer Testing.** (Test process to ensure that all requirements have been met.)

The new system was introduced and tested through a small pilot program on six delivery trucks. All support systems were fully tested.

7. **Transition.** (The process of putting the new or changed system into actual production usage.)

Over the course of the following year, the new system was fully implemented throughout the entire delivery fleet and across all existing systems.

Although it is difficult to attribute all of the company's revenue increases *fully* to the new system, there was a clearly measurable decrease in returned goods because of more effective shelf stocking. Additionally, a lease/purchasing plan allowed the project costs to be reduced to less than $1.4 million. Cost recovery was reduced to three years and the company continues to profit from the new system.

## System Test Plan

The *system test plan*, sometimes referred to as the *customer test plan*, is the final document to provide technical definition to the project during the planning stages. A system test plan describes the series of tests or walk-throughs, which will demonstrate for the customer that the new system performs its defined function(s). The test plans are developed based on the customer's requirements spelled out in the statement of work. These test plans are developed and expanded with the customer as the design process takes place. A development team should not proceed to construction of the system without a clearly defined system test plan.

System test plans are discussed in detail in Chapter Six, "Agree on Acceptance Criteria."

# Managing the Definition Process

### When to Define Each Phase in Detail

When a project manager is faced with the task of planning a project, it can seem overwhelming, particularly if he or she lacks management training or significant project management experience. It is easy to become lost in the sea of detail required. As a result, many project managers skip over vital aspects of planning, thereby guaranteeing problems and increasing the project's chances of failure. Frequent and continual pressure from customers and management to "get something going" further encourages the project manager to minimize the less tangible planning stages.

Planning is not a onetime event but an iterative process. Each successive phase demands varying forms of detail and definition. As presented in the previous section, the broad scope of the entire project is included within the statement of work. Each subsequent phase is defined in detail only as it is approached. The statement of work and detail definition of each ensuing phase is prepared as the final task of the preceding phase is completed. Since the true requirements for each phase are evident only from the preceding phase, the project manager should not attempt to define all phases in detail at the beginning of a project. This approach has proven itself impossible and inefficient.

Dividing a project into phases also helps ensure that the specific goals of each phase are not lost in the overall goals of the project. At Keane, we have learned the advantage of treating each phase not as part of a project, but rather as a project itself; therefore, all six principles of Productivity Management are applied to each phase.

## Involving the Extended Team in the Definition Process

During the definition phase, the project manager should involve everyone who has a significant and relevant interest in the project. The stereotypical programmer has trouble with such inclusion. Many of us gravitated toward information processing because it offered us an opportunity to control our destinies—at least on the job. Typically, if given a task, the information processor had great freedom to operate unilaterally. Whether it was a program to write, a screen to build, a report to lay out, or a system to design, the task was usually handled as an individual effort. When the individual's primary responsibility is that one task, he or she may not need to involve others. This is not the case for the project manager.

When this same technical person who prefers "doing his or her own thing" without interference from others has been promoted to project manager, the job is to get work from other people—and it can be an extremely rude awakening. He or she will sometimes find that there are people to depend on for support who really don't care too much about the project. Or that they simply have their own set of priorities and pressures more important to them than the project. For someone who has been used to "handling it" alone, managing a team can be a frustrating experience.

As a project manager, you must identify those people who have a level of involvement in the project and get them participating with you in the definition stage. Not only will you have a more accurately defined project because everyone has contributed, but the team will feel more of a personal investment in the final product.

While getting the team involved defining the job in detail, you should also get them committed to something concrete: to dates, or to hours of effort per week, or to percentage of time. Don't accept vague commitments along the lines of "Just call me when you need me, and I'll be right over." Definition is specific. Task them to completing deliverable products. The beginning of the project is your best opportunity for commitment. Once the project is under way, it is much more difficult to get and enforce these kinds of commitments.

## Resistance to the Planning Effort

Adequate time must be allotted to planning and ensuring that the project team and the customers agree on the project's scope and objectives. One of the first real hazards on a project is the impression that the team is wasting too much time up front with nothing really happening. They begin to feel the *WISCY* pressure—*"Why Isn't Someone Coding Yet?"*—which usually comes from customers and managers. Customers and managers almost always have tight schedules and strong desires to see something concrete right away. When they are accustomed to immediate results, it can be nerve-wracking for them to feel the "paralysis of analysis"—planning that goes on seemingly without end.

The customer often finds it difficult to pay for what is unseen. Nevertheless, he or she must be convinced of the absolute importance of adequate up-front planning. It is much easier and cheaper to change a piece of paper or two at the beginning than to reprogram and test later on. The industry has been saying it for years: One hour up front will save you ten hours out back.

Succumbing to WISCY pressure will result in shortcuts during the planning phases and costly premature programming. You've probably witnessed it: "They're in a hurry for this one, Sam. You start coding while Marie and I find out what they want!" Such planning "on the fly" inevitably creates a design lacking conceptual unity and a variety of problems that require considerably more time to repair on the back end than they would have required to prevent with up-front planning.

A pell-mell rush to get something—anything—done is one of the main causes of the notorious ***90% Done Syndrome.*** Before Keane developed and practiced the Principles of Productivity Management, we were somewhat amazed to note how quickly our projects were reported to be 90% done. This amazement eventually changed to panic when we realized that the final 10% of these projects seemed to contain 90% of the problems and, oddly enough, seemed to take as long—or longer—to finish as the first 90%.

Actually, it was only in the final 10% of the project that the problems were discovered. Or, more likely, the team had ignored them up to that point, hoping they would magically go away. We realized that statements like "We're 90% done, boss" weren't really telling us anything except that the project team had used up 90% of the time or money. We now measure completion by short-term deliverable products and actual effort hours expended and find that our results have improved significantly.

It is important to remember that the opportunity for up-front project definition does not come twice. There is probably no other single project management endeavor that will provide the rewards that adequate detailed project definition does. Resistance to thorough planning should be addressed and overridden at all costs.

## Selecting a Development Approach

The approach used to develop software will vary by type of project. The traditional waterfall approach (finish one phase completely before you proceed to the next) may be right for one project whereas a prototyping approach or perhaps a rapid iterative development approach may be right for another. All projects should not be structured to fit within a single approach.

For example, Keane is working on two projects for a large chemical company. For one project, we are using a prototyping approach because the project involves a new application of CASE technology to be used by a department that was recently formed to develop a photochemical product. No one involved in the project could define exactly what they wanted in advance, and prototyping provides incremental development that permits a gradual evolution of the system. The second project is for the department responsible for polystyrene intermediate products in the same company and uses a RAD (Rapid Application Development) approach. Use of RAD is a standard policy within that department because of the rapidly changing and highly competitive nature of the products they develop, produce, and market. In each case, the project's characteristics determined the best development approach.

The systems development life cycle should provide alternative approaches to guiding the manager and developers through the software building process. Keane's Frameworks for Software Development, a diagram of which appears in figure 1, provides specific approaches for the following software development processes:

- Traditional Waterfall Approach
- Rapid Application Development
- Client-Server Approach

Frameworks for the following approaches are under development:

- Prototyping
- Purchased packages
- CASE technology
- Object-oriented development

Each one of these software development approaches has a unique way of fitting into the systems development life cycle. Although there would be some crossover, by and large, each approach will have somewhat different phases, activities, tasks, and deliverables.

To some extent, the approach used will be dictated by the tools at your disposal. If your organization has not invested the considerable time and money in purchasing and learning CASE technology, it would probably be the wrong choice for your next hot project. Many of the approaches, however, are not tool dependent but are only *procedure* dependent. The best approach is based on customer requirements, overall organizational goals, resource availability, and other considerations that can greatly increase the success and effectiveness of the project.

A complete discussion on how to select the right approach for developing a system is beyond the scope of this book on project management. Effective project management, however, demands that there be an awareness of alternative methods for software development. Each approach defines a somewhat varying set of activities, sequences, and deliverable products. These activities, sequences, and deliverable products must be clearly defined and agreed upon by all parties involved to ensure successful definition—and completion—of the project.

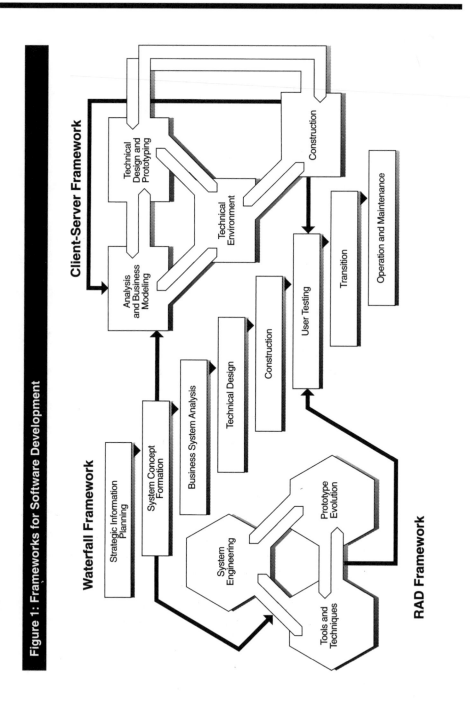

Figure 1: Frameworks for Software Development

**Client-Server Framework**

- Technical Design and Prototyping
- Analysis and Business Modeling
- Technical Environment
- Construction

**Waterfall Framework**

- Strategic Information Planning
- System Concept Formation
- Business System Analysis
- Technical Design
- Construction
- User Testing
- Transition
- Operation and Maintenance

**RAD Framework**

- System Engineering
- Prototype Evolution
- Tools and Techniques

## Defining Project Success and Failure

Part of the definition process should be devoted to identifying what will constitute success or failure of the project. In some instances, the entire success of the project may be predicated on meeting the deadline. In other instances, the need to stay within a certain cost range is more critical. But there are frequently other, more important reasons than simple date and budget parameters. Below is a sample list of critical success elements drawn from many different projects:

- The project is on time.

- The project is within budget.

- The project meets customer requirements.

- The project meets customer expectations.

- The project fits within the organizational, divisional, or departmental visions and business strategy.

- The project offers an effective training exercise in a new technology.

- The project develops the skills of the project manager.

- The project achieves a level of profit on the outputs.

- The project enables the customer to provide a higher level of customer service.

- The project keeps staff occupied.

- The project reduces business costs.

You should develop a list that is relevant to your organization or project and add to it as more elements occur to you.

Choosing from such a list is a helpful starting point for customers and managers at the beginning of a project. The temptation, of course, is to claim that *all* items are important and vital to the success of the project. The problem with such a scenario is that some of the items are in direct conflict with others. Pick one or perhaps two critical success factors and prioritize them in clear sequence. Then, when push comes to shove, you can turn to a very short list and say, "Budget takes precedence." Coming to this mutual decision early in the project will help maintain progress later on when the battle is more heated, and rational decisions seem more difficult to come by. At the end of a project, examining the selected criteria will help you evaluate the success or failure of the project.

## Varying Levels of Detail Definition

Defining the job in detail can mean different things depending on where you are in the project. In a project's early stages when the customer or management wants a "rough" estimate, project definition is less detailed than at later stages when you are scheduling people, tasks, and completion dates. More accurate and detailed definition takes time.

You often will have to provide early estimates for customers or for internal Information Systems groups. Customers frequently want some kind of a "ballpark estimate" as quickly as possible so they can decide whether to pursue the project any further, to look for alternatives, or to scrap the whole thing. The request for such a ballpark estimate calls for an abbreviated form of definition. There are automated tools that are helpful in these circumstances, which are described in the section, "Automated Tools," later in this chapter.

Over the course of a typical project, there are three separate levels of definition: *proposal, statement of work,* and *resource scheduling*.

1. The *proposal* is for the customer who needs a form of quick definition, approach, and estimates, usually to help in a feasibility determination. They are asking, "Is the project worth pursuing?"

2. The ***statement of work***, as previously described, is the most meaningful definition of the project, where the project manager will determine customer requirements and gain a thorough understanding of the project environment. He or she will also establish a time and cost estimate for the project at this stage. Planning and definition from the statement of work usually give the customer enough information to approve the project.

3. ***Resource scheduling*** is the most detailed level of definition, where the project is broken into pieces or phases and assigned to resources (individuals or teams). Each phase will have a specific deliverable product (or products) at its conclusion. This level of detail definition is usually done on what we call a ***90-day rolling window***, which refers to the immediate three future months of a project. It would be an unreasonable waste of time to try to plan an entire, lengthy project at the level of resource scheduling at its beginning; but at any given time, at least three future months of the project should be resource scheduled. Chapter 4, "Break the Job Down Using the 80-Hour Rule," covers resource scheduling in greater detail.

## Estimating Time and Costs of the Definition Effort

Defining the job in detail takes time and effort, which of course also means money. That time, effort, and money must be tracked. Below is a guide for how to account for the three levels of project definition.

**Proposal.** Some proposals are sheer flights of fancy for customers and do not necessarily represent serious systems development effort. An organization might request a proposal to corroborate their own or someone else's estimate of a job. In any case, you need to make an independent judgment call on whether a request for a proposal is real or not.

At Keane, if a project opportunity seems sincere, we first decide whether we have the skills and resources to handle it. We then estimate the time and resources appropriate to invest in the proposal and stick to that estimate. At this early stage, we will usually only prepare a range estimate (worst case to best case) of the project's ultimate cost. Not until we complete detailed definition in a finalized statement of work as noted below, will we commit to a specific cost estimate.

Keane usually does not charge time to a project for proposal definition. This is a marketing effort, and cumulative time involved in proposal activities is reflected in our general rate structure; however, an organization must make some sort of evaluative judgment on each case. Whether to charge for a proposal is ultimately a business decision for each organization to consider closely.

**Statement of Work.** Any time spent preparing a statement of work and all its attendant parts (background, scope, project plans, final estimates, acceptance criteria, etc.) *is* charged to the project. This is clearly a necessary step in planning any project, and not to reflect it in a time and cost estimate is simply an incorrect approach to project management. With the statement of work, we are usually willing to commit to a firm estimate for the phase being defined and provide a refined range estimate for the entire project. It is unlikely that we would make a time or price commitment for the remainder of the project unless the project was small, well structured and well defined.

**Resource Scheduling.** All time for the detailed definition that will produce the resource schedules is also charged to the project. This is a continuing effort occurring throughout the life of the project, and line item entries in the work breakdown should reflect resource scheduling as a recurring task.

## Checklists

Perhaps one of the most reliable and simple ways of defining and tracking progress is a checklist. Architects have voluminous checklists because experience has taught them the consequences of not using them. A glaring example: In a multimillion dollar building nearing completion, the architects realized that they had overlooked required reinforced walls in the elevator shafts. This item would have been readily apparent from even a cursory checklist. Had this oversight been discovered during the planning stages, the correction could have been done on paper. As it turned out, a sum of several million dollars was required to repair the error. Parallel examples abound in Information Systems development. Detecting errors at their point of origin rather than during testing simplifies correction and saves time and money exponentially.

## Quality Assurance in Definition

The project manager must ensure that quality assurance is built into the project and that time is allotted for it from the outset. Quality checks should be scheduled throughout the project and identified in the work breakdown in their many forms: inspections, walk-throughs, reviews, potential problem analyses, etc.

Quality Assurance will be discussed in detail in Chapter 4, "Break the Job Down Using the 80-Hour Rule."

## Automated Tools: Project Management

There are myriad software packages available to help manage projects. Some will run on the smallest notebooks, others demand the horsepower of a large mainframe computer. Most projects can be effectively managed with software that will run on a medium-sized PC and will provide you the ability to do all the planning, tracking, and forecasting you need.

Typically, the project manager will use the software to build the work breakdown structure, to apply the estimates for the various tasks, to assign resources, to schedule the completion of tasks, to report and track actual progress against the activities, and to make forecasts and estimates as changes demand. Once the basic project information is initially plugged into the software, managing change is greatly simplified.

The software eases the burden of identifying task dependencies and setting up the *critical path.* The critical path is the path of dependent activities that represents the shortest time in which the project can be completed. Having the critical path well defined provides a focus for project management control. If any one activity on that path slips, then the date of project completion will be delayed. Consequently, all tasks and activities must be very carefully managed. It is very difficult to identify the critical path manually and some form of automation is extremely helpful in dealing with the complexities of interdependent tasks.

Several vendors now offer products intended to expedite the project management process in its earliest phases. Based on parametric data that you provide relevant to size, risk, complexity, etc., the software will profile your project and suggest an approach and an appropriate work breakdown structure. It will also generate time and cost estimates for individual phases or for the entire project, develop schedules by resource, and prepare detailed project plans. Once an initial plan or proposal is agreed upon, the software will develop detailed project planning to virtually any level desired. An example of a Gantt Chart generated by project management software appears in exhibit 2.

Keane has found these modeling products valuable in developing initial proposals to customers. After completing an appropriate amount of up-front analysis, we can develop useful project proposals in three to four hours using automated packages. And of course, they are immensely easier to change should it become necessary, since the estimates and tasks can

## Exhibit 2: Phased Approach Gantt Chart

| Name | Est. Hrs. | Res. List | April 4 | 11 | 18 | 25 | May 2 | 9 | 16 | 23 |
|---|---|---|---|---|---|---|---|---|---|---|
| **Business System Analysis** | | | | | | | | | | |
| **Project Management** | | | | | | | | | | |
| Develop Project Plan/Schedule | 32 | PM | | | | | | | | |
| Manage the Project | 300 | PM | | | | | | | | |
| **Prepare Diagrams** | | | | | | | | | | |
| Develop the Data Model | 240 | BA CB | | | | | | | | |
| Develop the Process Model | 292 | BA CB | | | | | | | | |
| **Generate Functional/Data Reqmnts.** | | | | | | | | | | |
| Write the Primitive Process Specifications | 450 | BA CB C | | | | | | | | |
| Generate the Data Dictionary | 260 | CT | | | | | | | | |
| Reconcile the Process and Data Models | 168 | BA CT C | | | | | | | | |
| **Generate Performance Reqmnts.** | | | | | | | | | | |
| Estimate Performance Requirements | 160 | CB BA C | | | | | | | | |
| Update the Data Model | 96 | BA CB C | | | | | | | | |
| **Produce User Reqmnts. Document** | | | | | | | | | | |
| Gather System Specifications | 276 | BA CB C | | | | | | | | |
| Distribute the Draft Specifications | 32 | BA CT | | | | | | | | |
| **Assess Implementation Reqmnts.** | | | | | | | | | | |
| Assess Technical Issues | 96 | PM BA | | | | | | | | |
| Determine Design Approach | 64 | PM BA | | | | | | | | |
| **User Review of Requirements** | | | | | | | | | | |
| Prepare for User Reviews | 96 | BA PM | | | | | | | | |
| Conduct User Reviews | 112 | BA CM | | | | | | | | |
| **Decide Changes & Impl. Strategy** | | | | | | | | | | |
| Accept User Changes | 128 | PM BA | | | | | | | | |
| Document Sponsor Decisions | 32 | BA CB | | | | | | | | |
| **Plan Technical Design Phase** | | | | | | | | | | |
| Develop the Technical Design Plan | 140 | PM BA | | | | | | | | |
| BSA Complete | | | | | | | | | | |
| Project Manager | 8 | PM | 32.0 | 25.0 | 25.0 | 25.0 | 25.0 | 25.0 | 25.0 | 25.0 |
| Business Analyst | 8 | BA | 32.0 | 40.0 | 40.0 | 40.0 | 40.0 | 40.0 | 40.0 | 40.0 |
| Customer Business Expert | 8 | CB | 32.0 | 40.0 | 40.0 | 40.0 | 40.0 | 40.0 | 40.0 | 40.0 |
| Consultants - Technical | 8 | CT | 32.0 | 40.0 | 40.0 | 40.0 | 40.0 | 40.0 | 40.0 | 40.0 |
| Customer Manager | 8 | CM | 2.0 | 2.5 | 2.5 | 2.5 | 2.5 | 2.5 | 2.5 | 2.5 |
| Customer Users | 8 | CU | 1.6 | 2.0 | 2.0 | 1.5 | 1.5 | 1.5 | 1.5 | 1.5 |
| TEAM | 8 | TEAM | | | | | | | | |
| Totals | | | 131.6 | 149.5 | 149.5 | 149.0 | 149.0 | 149.0 | 149.0 | 149.0 |

be modified at any point throughout the process. While they do not in any way replace the need for thorough analysis and skilled resources, we do find that they can make a significant contribution to the overall project definition and management process.

## Automated Tools: Technical Definition

The project manager should give careful consideration to what automated tools he or she will use to help define, analyze, design, develop, program, and manage a project. There is a never-ending array of software to help define requirements, analyze business needs, design systems, program, test, and manage the systems development process. The cost estimates, schedules, and deliverable products will, to some extent, be dependent on these tools used; therefore, the tools should be identified during the definition process.

A few examples of development activities that automated software will now perform follows:

- Provide a model of the current system through charts, diagrams, pictures, and narratives
- Provide a model of the proposed system through the same formats
- Generate pseudo-code or executable code from various design documents
- Create system test plans
- Generate customer documentation

Any combination of this software might be employed within the various approaches for systems development; that is, the standard waterfall approach, prototyping, or rapid application development all could be implemented using software. The project manager must be aware of the software aids being used, and exercise appropriate management control over the resultant deliverable products.

Beware, however. One of the main considerations often overlooked by project managers is training in the use of new software technology. Inevitably, some training costs and time must be borne by the project itself. Do not simply assume that the efficient use of an automated tool will be "picked up" over the course of the project without a learning curve.

## Chapter Summary: Define the Job in Detail

1. Make sure that the activity with which you are involved meets the definition of a project before trying to apply project management principles to it.

2. A project usually begins at the Requirements Definition phase.

3. Definition must be in writing to ensure mutual understanding and commitment.

4. The three major documents of definition are the statement of work, the work breakdown structure derived from the systems development life cycle, and the system test plan.

5. The statement of work describes the environment or "spirit" of the project.

6. The work breakdown structure and the system test plan identify the technical issues of the project.

7. The statement of work will ensure that the project team

   a. understands the problem, opportunity or need;

   b. has an approach to meeting the opportunity or problem; and

   c. can provide a fair estimate of the time and cost.

8. Project definition involves breaking the project into small, manageable pieces.

9. A separate statement of work should be prepared for each phase of a project. Each phase should be managed as a separate project.

10. The system test plan describes how the customer will test the deliverables of the project to ensure that they meet their specifications and expectations.

11. All parties having significant involvement in the project should participate in the definition, planning, estimating, and control. The customers are clearly a part of the extended project team.

12. Projects should be reviewed to decide which developmental approach to use.

13. What constitutes project success must be identified during this definition stage in order to make appropriate evaluation at completion.

14. Because increasing details of definition require more time and money, the appropriate level of definition should be decided at the very beginning of the project activity.

15. Quality assurance must be built into the project from the very beginning by providing time and tasks for quality checks.

16. There is a great deal of automated project management software that can aid the definition process.

# 2

## Principle Two:
## Get the Right People Involved

# Get the Right People Involved

Projects seem to go rather well until people get involved in them. With people come personalities, ambitions, egos, drive, needs, and habits, all of which make project management an activity of many unpredictable variables. The project manager who has the right approach to people, however, will be able to lead them through any technical challenge that might arise. For that reason, the Principles of Productivity Management emphasize the management and leadership of *people*. At Keane, we like to turn the common axiom "Projects don't fail, people do" into the more optimistic "Projects don't succeed, people do."

When managed properly, involving people can create some of the true successes and rewards of project management. Project management offers a distinct opportunity for growth, personal accomplishment, interpersonal working relationships, challenge, and financial rewards for you, the project team, and your organization.

## The Team

### Recognizing the Extended Team

Chapter 1 emphasized the importance of defining the environmental characteristics of a project. Much of the environment is created by the people involved, and the project manager must understand all of the interrelationships within the customer organization, the project team(s), Information Systems, and other technical and administrative support groups, vendors, and any other people who can affect the project. This group of people linked by the existence of the project is known as the *extended team*. Recognizing each member of this team is vital to the success of the project, and the project manager must do all that is necessary to direct the extended team toward a common objective.

Undermanaging the people and overcontrolling the project is a common problem. Many project managers can tell you within a dollar or an hour how late and over budget a project is but seem unable to do much about it. The project seems to be controlling them. Managers sometimes try to tame projects with plotter-produced, four-color Gantt charts that stretch two-thirds of the way around a room. They have everyone reporting activity down to half-hour segments, and they produce daily status reports, forecasts and analyses that dutifully predict project-, phase-, and task-completion dates. These methods are useful, but the project manager's focus must be on the people involved.

The major goals of this second principle, Get the Right People Involved, are

- To understand the roles and responsibilities of the extended team members

- To establish effective communication between all individuals involved in the project

- To emphasize the importance of gaining involvement and commitment from the entire team

- To motivate the extended team to achieve the project's goals.

## Assembling the Development Team

When you undertake a new project, naturally you want the very best people on your team. Unfortunately, this is not always possible. The most qualified people seem to have a way of already being on someone else's project, and usually what ends up making an individual "right" for a project is *availability*. If you are just starting a three-person project for your organization, and there are three people sitting on the bench, guess who the right people for your project are likely to be. One can only hope they will not be Larry, Moe, and Curly. In those cases, you must evaluate the skill level of the people available to see if they meet the minimum requirements of the project. As long as you know in advance what to expect from the project, you can make appropriate plans according to the skills of the people available. If the project team must be staffed with less experienced people, recognize that you can still successfully complete the project—it just may take a little longer.

Since the right people always seem to be working on another project, the people you have must become the right people. If you only ran projects with the right people, you would manage very few projects. Perhaps the more appropriate—if more awkward—title for this principle is "Involve the People You Have, Rightly." You are better off getting the people you have rightly, than spending an inordinate amount of time trying to put together a perfect project team.

A serious problem arises when the ability of the project team is lower than what you originally assumed and planned for in the estimate. The project team may not be in place at the time of the estimate, or reassignment and turnover may alter the composition of the original team. Because an organization frequently experiences conflicting demands for its staff, it is not unusual for a project manager to discover that a higher-priority project has usurped some of his or her previously guaranteed resources. In these rude but real cases, the project manager must convince management that either the time, the cost, and/or the project scope have to be adjusted. Too many project managers in such cases continue to trip along with the same plan as if nothing has changed. The result is a no-win situation for the manager and everyone on the team, and life becomes increasingly depressing as the impossible deadline approaches. When a variable as important as the ability or quantity of resources on the project team changes, the project manager should reassess what the project team is realistically capable of delivering.

What adjustments are made will depend on project priorities. A systems development project can almost always be prioritized using three criteria:

- Delivering a system of a given scope and functionality
- Delivering the system within the original budget
- Delivering the system by a given date

We often see these criteria presented in the triangle shown in figure 2.

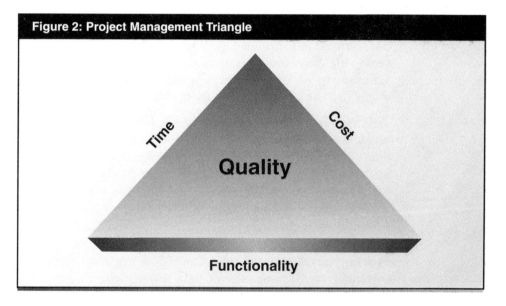

**Figure 2: Project Management Triangle**

Time
Cost
Quality
Functionality

If you alter the length of one side of the triangle, something must change in one or both of the other sides. If you lose staff, for example, then more time must be allotted or the scope of the system must be reduced accordingly. If you have identified the highest priorities and objectives of the project as discussed in Chapter 1, these decisions will be easier to make.

Project managers these days have less and less control over the makeup of their project team. Primarily at fault is the matrix-like personnel structure that pulls resources from many different groups and organizations to work on a single project. "Right sizing," where organizations are using fewer resources with greater effectiveness, also contributes. The effect is that project managers will continue to have less say in who is involved in their projects, but will, of course, be expected to continue to perform effectively. Managing them properly is the only way to achieve consistent effectiveness with a varying team.

## Setting Goals as a Team

The success of a project hinges on the development team's endorsement of the project goals. If the team participates in setting the goals, they feel heightened responsibility for achieving them. You may be surprised by how hard a team works to meet a deadline they themselves fixed.

True team participation also provides valuable input for the project manager. He or she can be confident that the goals are realistic if everyone on the team has participated in setting them. The project's goals will also be more likely understood by all team members from the beginning. When everyone is confident that individual goals, as well as project goals, can be achieved, project morale becomes a positive force unlikely to be undermined by the "It can't be done" syndrome. The more each individual owns the project and his or her tasks in it, the more investment he or she will make toward achieving the project's goals.

## Team Motivation

It is perhaps unrealistic to expect everyone on a team to identify with and develop loyalty to a project. People on a well-managed project, however, are very likely to identify with and develop loyalty to the other people on their team. Any study of war heroes reveals that most of them perform life-threatening acts because they identified not with the high cause of the war effort but with their buddies in the unit. People on a project team will strive to perform in order not to let down their coworkers. This trait is important to keep in mind for team motivation.

Maslow's "Hierarchy of Needs" is a helpful tool for outlining a detailed evaluation of how to best motivate the project team. Maslow found that the lower level needs in the hierarchy are motivators until they are satisfied, and then one must look to a higher level need for motivation. The successful project manager must assess the individual performers' needs and provide the appropriate level of motivation. Each need in Maslow's hierarchy has some relevance to a manager's approach to the project team.

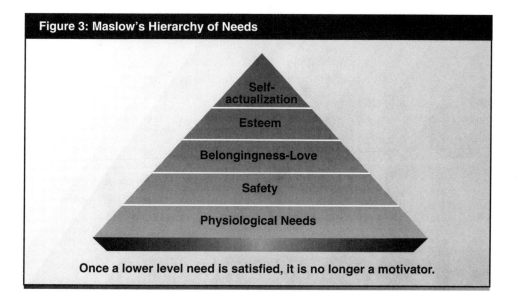

**Figure 3: Maslow's Hierarchy of Needs**

Self-actualization

Esteem

Belongingness-Love

Safety

Physiological Needs

**Once a lower level need is satisfied, it is no longer a motivator.**

*Physiological Needs* (the basic survival needs of food, clothing, and shelter). Although they may not be fulfilling an actual need, pizza and donuts are surprisingly effective motivators. Bring your team donuts every Thursday or Friday morning and pizza sometime every two weeks to a month, and they will appreciate it. The main thing, of course, is to do *something*.

*Safety.* Project team members have fears about jobs, group acceptance, meeting deadlines, maintaining technical currency, etc., and, though the fears may not be life threatening, they are real. Team members need to feel safe within the environment of their project, and the project manager must provide a net of safety. You do that by not repeating corporate rumors, by continually emphasizing the importance and value of what the team is doing, by assigning constructive work as soon as an individual becomes available, by protecting and standing up for your project team. Although the project and its team are hardly immune to the political and economic swirl, you must be very careful not to let them get caught up in it. Make sure that they stay focused on doing the job at hand.

***Belongingness and love.*** Belongingness is part and parcel of project management responsibility. The entire "team" concept is based on belongingness. A team is a synergistically powerful force for accomplishing a specific task, and it is your job to build and maintain that force.

Listed below are several basic team building measures that we use at Keane:

1. Create a document in organizational chart format that identifies all players on the team and their roles and responsibilities. See that everyone has a copy of this document.

2. At the very earliest opportunity, schedule a team meeting and have everyone attend.

3. Schedule and hold regular management-oriented team meetings. Do not let more than two weeks pass between meetings, and limit the meetings to one hour. These are nontechnical meetings; if there are technical problems to be addressed, schedule a separate meeting and involve only those whose presence is necessary.

4. As a project manager, do not feel compelled to control each team meeting. It can be beneficial to vary the meeting leadership among the team members and assign a different person to run each session.

5. It helps the project team to have a distinctive name. You may want to make that an assignment of the first team meeting.

6. Provide some product that identifies the team. No matter how trivial it may seem, you will be surprised by how such tokens are appreciated. We frequently use coffee mugs with everyone's names on them. Other options are caps, pens, notepads, distinctive binders, etc. Use your imagination and do something.

7. Schedule some sort of function every month or every other month. It could be a breakfast seminar, a lunch or dinner, a ball game. Again, almost anything will be appreciated.

*Esteem.* The team members need to feel good about what they are doing and believe that they are doing a good job. It is clearly the project manager's responsibility to make this happen. Good performance must be recognized and poor performance cannot be tolerated.

*Self-actualization.* A project manager must provide an environment in which the various team members can set and achieve their own goals. The individual will then determine what success means for him or her and will put together a plan to achieve that success.

We recommend assigning relatively significant blocks of work to people and asking them to develop schedules for completing the work. The schedules are then *their* plans, and the likelihood of them meeting their own plans is much higher than the likelihood of them meeting a plan that you have imposed on them. This concept is discussed in detail in Chapter 4, "Break the Job Down Using the 80-Hour Rule."

Notice that fear and greed are not on Maslow's list—though some project managers have tried to add them in the past. The admonition, "Do a good job on this project or get fired," may work at first, but tends not to last very long. The problem with it is that actually getting someone fired for alleged poor performance is rare. And often, the poor performer is simply not rightly involved in the project and would be unfairly terminated with such action. Appealing to greed may work a little better, but even the best carrot just doesn't have the power to motivate throughout the life of a project.

Most people—especially information technologists—truly care about the work they do. Few set out to be the most marginal performer a company has ever seen. People want to do a good job, and they want someone to tell them they are doing a good job. The project manager needs to provide or create that recognition.

Appropriate and satisfying recognition differs from person to person. Different people have different WIIFMs: *"What's In It For Me?"* (pronounced *wif-ims*). Each member of the extended team needs to perceive some attainable "win" by being involved with a project. Some need only the most infrequent and oblique attention. Others need public recognition, perhaps through regular mentions of their successes in memos and team meetings. For some, learning a new technology is a big WIIFM. For others the reward may be an opportunity to teach others, or a chance to do a bit of management as a project leader. Realize that you will never be 100% successful in motivating people, but instilling team members with personal pride in their work will maximize success.

## Team Morale

The success of a project team is based on more than the skills and talents of the individuals who make up the team. Sustained morale is another crucial factor. How well the team works together, its cohesiveness, its ability to communicate, and the motivation the individuals have toward the group's goals are all factors that add to high morale. Beware, however: high morale can be quickly eroded by dissension, self-centeredness, finger pointing and poor communication.

The project manager can create a positive environment by encouraging honesty and openness among team members, and between team members and the project manager. Team members should be encouraged to communicate all problems to their manager. Problems should be treated as opportunities for team members to develop leadership, to improve the system, and to exercise their creativity. Frequent team meetings in which people are encouraged to discuss problems as well as their progress encourages open communication among project participants. Regular and frequent walk-throughs or inspections demonstrate the attention of a project manager and also help to ensure a focus on the ultimate goal of the project.

On a recent project at Keane, a project manager gave two team members some freedom to demonstrate problem-solving leadership skills. The project team was having a difficult time programming complex automatic inventory ordering and forecasting routines for a high-volume automotive parts supplier. The project manager suggested that the senior analyst and senior programmer, who got along quite well, focus on the problem for two days working at one of their homes instead of coming into the office. They jumped at the opportunity to avoid two days of commuting and to work uninterrupted. When they returned the following Thursday, not only did they have a creative and effective solution to the problem, but they had pseudo-coded all the programs as well. When appropriate, such freedom can generate startling results.

*Feedback* is also a critical ingredient for high morale. No one should feel like an anonymous contributor to a project's success. The project manager should constantly offer positive feedback to team members. People simply want to know, "Am I doing a good job, and if not, tell me what I can do to fix it."

## Project Team Organization

"How do I organize my project team most effectively?" The answer to this pervasive question is … it depends. It depends on the nature of the project. It depends on where the project stands in the systems development life cycle. It depends on the software being developed. On the people involved. On the mood of management. On the critical success factors of the project. On the vision of the organization.

We find it increasingly inappropriate to attempt to identify a singular project team approach for every systems development process. It is better to gain experience with several approaches and spend conscious effort up front agreeing on the approach that will be most effective in each instance.

Empowered or participative management of project teams is currently in vogue. Many organizations struggle to make this work, but there are many employees who do not want to be empowered or for whom it is not an appropriate fit. These are not bad people. They simply want to come to work in the morning, bury themselves in meaningful work and go home at a reasonable time. Others find such regular schedules stifling and are at their best when energetically involved in the dynamics of group problem solving, goal setting, and decision making. The great mistake is to draw general conclusions and to pound all people into the same holes.

The project manager and all senior members of the project team must decide in advance how they want to structure the team on an effort. There is a broad range of team organizations available. Choose one, and if it does not work, *change it.* It is absurd to try to push forward with a flawed arrangement.

## The Customer

### Client/Customer/User Relations

Involving people rightly applies not only to the development team; team spirit should extend to the customer. Unfortunately, it often does not, and when projects run into trouble, project personnel like to blame customers:

- Customers didn't adequately define their needs.

- Customers frequently changed their mind.

- Customers didn't provide the backup services they should have.

- Customers didn't know what they wanted in the first place.

Customers are as much a part of the project team as any software developer; as such, the customer should be treated with the same importance and respect as the rest of the team. When segregation occurs, the project manager has usually failed to carefully evaluate the customer environment and to involve people rightly in the project. What may seem to be a problem with the customers or with other members of the extended team is often a failure to work closely with everyone and to understand their concerns. Ultimately, fostering the relationship with the customer and other extended team members is the project manager's responsibility.

Of course, you will usually find that the customers' major concerns are not with the project, but rather with getting their own jobs done first. This is exactly as it should be. A new project frequently requires the time of people who already feel the insistent demands of their full-time jobs—jobs which, incidentally, they intend to keep long after the project is completed. Customer personnel are often not available when their input is needed for the project. A project manager must walk a narrow path in getting commitments honored yet maintaining flexibility to the customer's business demands.

At Keane, we were once installing an integrated general shipping and returns system for a regional home shopping network. The system required a fair amount of interface with the accounting group which was not going well. The problems were that 1) it seemed very difficult for us to get accurate and timely information, 2) gaining acceptance for completed deliverable products with accounting connections seemed to take forever, and 3) the deliverables were endlessly nitpicked.

The problem was our relationship with Harry, a quiet and conscientious, longtime accounting clerk. He had been given the additional duty of minor surveillance over our work on the new system. We treated Harry rather casually and simply mailed material to him or just dropped it on his desk as we passed by. What we failed to realize was that Harry took his job very seriously, worried endlessly both on and off the job about what we were doing, and agonized over everything we gave him.

Once we recognized the oversight on our part, we began inviting Harry to participate in our team meetings. We then had him give a presentation on how our work affected the accounting group. After a short time, he became an active, recognized member of the project team, and our dealings with accounting improved remarkably. Harry relished his augmented role, and his managers formally appointed him chief liaison to Information Systems for the shipping and returns system.

As Harry came to fully understand what we were doing and as we understood his concerns, the whole picture changed for the better. Harry became committed to helping get the system going, and we helped Harry get warranted recognition from his manager.

Once again, it is unlikely that a project will fail because of a technical problem. Poor interpersonal relationships, political pressures, organizational changes and attitudes, and customer neglect, however, can cause a project's rapid demise.

## Multi-Customer Projects

Multi-customer projects present another potential client relations problem. These are the projects that cross the organizational boundaries of several different departments or divisions. The more people involved in a project, the less likely they are to agree. How do you meet the often conflicting needs of many customers? Who has the authority to make decisions? Who is to be the arbiter?

Similar problems can arise when the person or department who authorizes and pays for the project is different from the one(s) who will use the system. The user's desire for more functions may conflict with management's desire to limit the project's budget.

The project manager must be aware of all parties involved on the customer's end and must determine the best way to navigate the accompanying politics.

## Who Should Manage the Project?

Generally speaking, the customer should manage the project, mainly because they have the most vested, long-term interests. This may not always be convenient or possible, however, and each organization must address this issue project by project. There are circumstances in which the entire effort is best managed by the Information Systems project manager. (Of course, a single project manager within the Information Systems organization should manage the technical effort.)

Technical teams reluctant to hand over the reins tend to supply the following list of reasons why the customer should not manage the project:

1. The customers don't really know what they want.

2. The customers don't have project management experience.

3. The customers don't have the information technology experience to define their requirements.

While those comments may be accurate, there are also problems involved with assigning the management responsibility to the Information Systems organization.

1. Information Systems also do not know what the customer wants. They only *think* they know, which is even worse.

2. It may be true—unfortunately—that the customers do not have project management experience. But they *should* have that experience, and now is the time for them to get it.

3. Customers do not necessarily need a lot of information technology experience to manage the project. They need expertise in their functional business areas and broad management experience. Properly done requirements definition should be free of any proposed solution ... computer based or not. (As a brief aside, most customers and clients now have a pretty good conceptual understanding of information technology. It's a different—and more informed—world than 25 years ago.)

The system and software will soon be turned over to the customers to run their business applications. They are the owners and as such should assume management responsibility if at all possible.

## Customer Roles and Responsibilities

Customers should be involved as much as they are willing and where their presence will most contribute, but it is at *acceptance* that customer involvement is absolutely crucial. One individual in the customer organization should assume responsibility for the acceptance function, preferably someone who has final decision-making authority over the project. Whatever the level of customer involvement, both customer and developer should agree on it in advance. Ultimately, the project manager should determine the most appropriate techniques for ensuring customer involvement.

## Involving Customer Senior Management

Frequently, senior management approves a project and then leaves the system developer with a member of the customer organization whose sole aim seems to be to redefine the project. This is a difficult position to be in if you are a project manager expected to bring a project to a profitable conclusion.

As project manager, your goal should be to garner the highest level of support from senior management with the lowest level of annoyance to them. If possible, a single individual with authority over the final product should attend major project reviews, review progress reports, participate in update sessions, and be willing to help resolve problems. Without such senior management involvement, you run the risk of finishing a project only to have the person with real authority step in and say, "This is all wrong. This is not what I wanted."

It is worth noting that the senior manager should be someone who can say yes as well as no. It is easy to say no, and often takes little or no evaluation of the situation. "No, you can't have any more money." "No, there is no more time." To say yes, however, implies that the manager has studied the problem and is making a conscious decision which he or she will defend later on.

At the very least, the project manager should gain the visible support of a key management person who has *influence* to resolve customer differences. This person is often referred to as a **sponsor.** On smaller projects, the sponsor may be the customer manager or department head, but on larger or strategic projects it could be someone outside the immediate project arena. Regardless of who it is, the sponsor should be someone who believes in the value of the project and is willing to help achieve success.

On many projects a customer representative or **liaison** is appointed to handle daily issues. When the direct involvement of a high-level manager cannot be arranged, this liaison assumes the additional responsibility of making management decisions. Although the liaison is an acceptable alternative, every attempt should be made to get the relevant manager involved as well. Consider, for instance, a multi-customer project whose project scope must be reduced to meet a date deadline. Who decides which customer departments will lose functions? Who tells them, and—more important—who makes the decisions stick? No project is problem free, and the inevitable problems that arise are often impossible to resolve unless a high-level manager is involved.

If all efforts to involve a senior manager fail, and customer interface will be solely through an appointed liaison, the project manager should identify the charter of this individual. How much authority does he or she have to make decisions and to resolve problems? Is he or she able and willing to "draw the line" so the system and its budget don't grow too large? Under what circumstances should the project manager consult higher-level management? Most important, does the representative have the authority to approve the entire system, or has the senior manager reserved final approval authority? The time to think about these matters is at the beginning of the project, not later when crisis occurs.

## Helping the Customer Adjust to a New System

Change affects the power structure of an organization. Change brought about by a new system can sometimes result in a zero-sum situation: one person's gain is another's loss. Some people may see a new system as a threat to their jobs or perhaps as an increase in their workload with no increase in responsibility or pay. Cooperation can be difficult to obtain from those people who expect to be adversely affected by a successfully completed project. The project manager needs to be aware of the politics in a customer organization—all organizations are political to some degree—and of the political *effect* of the new system. Whose job will be affected and how? Will the new system give more responsibility to one person or department at the expense of any others?

Projects that break new ground are most likely to wreak havoc within the customer organization, especially in departments with systems that have seen little recent change. If a system is going to change the status quo, or is even *perceived* as such, the customers who feel threatened can and sometimes do "stonewall" the project. The more change a system creates, the more the change will be resisted. Understandably: when you know all the shortcuts on the existing system, you don't want to become an instant neophyte on a new one. It is essential that the customers recognize the benefits of the new system, and that the project manager maintain an ongoing campaign to help them see those benefits.

## The Project Manager

Perhaps the most daunting question on the subject of getting the right people involved is *Are you the right project manager for the job?* Do you have enough experience? Are you intelligent enough? Do you have the technical skills? Do you have the management skills and stamina for an effort of this magnitude? There is the possibility that under closer scrutiny, some may suggest that you are not the "right" person to manage a given project; nevertheless, here you are doing it. Self-doubt aside, you must make yourself the right person. Getting everyone involved rightly also refers to you, the project manager. If you have failed to put yourself in a winning mind-set, it is unlikely that you will be able to inspire the rest of the team. The most successful project manager is one who keeps the path clear for the team to proceed at their own pace. With that attitude in place, you proceed to specifics.

*The Project Manager's role is to clear the way, so the team can do their job.*

## Project Manager Job Functions and Tasks

In order to determine the specific roles and responsibilities of a typical project manager, Keane employed the services of a highly regarded behavioral research firm. They conducted *behavioral event interviews* with a number of Keane's best project managers as well as those from other organizations outside of our company. Their behavior analysts then detailed what project managers do and why some of them do it better than others. The result was the construction of a "superior project manager" model to strive for in our manager selection and training.

The list in exhibit 3 identifies the principal tasks that the project manager performs. The order and grouping is not set in stone, but the list has proven a useful road map for managers at Keane. It is broken into *job functions* then, more specifically, into *tasks* that fall within each job function.

Note that the project managers do not actually have to *do* all tasks themselves, but they do have to see that the tasks are done by someone.

---

**Exhibit 3: Project Manager Job Functions and Tasks**

### 1. Planning

- Analyze client interview data for objectives, deliverables, schedule, and environment assessment
- Analyze project for technical and environmental aspects
- Apply Principles of Productivity Management
- Determine people and resources needed for project
- Assign tasks to people
- Estimate costs, time, schedule
- Write and present project plan

### 2. Managing Tasks

- Estimate, validate, reestimate (as needed) project time, schedules
- Apply technical knowledge to project

---

**Exhibit 3 (continued)**

- Check on project status
- Maintain overview of project and its position/relationships in the larger system
- Maintain Project Control Book
- Prepare written status reports
- Track project changes
- Conduct project audits, walk-throughs
- Test project deliverables

### 3. Managing Project Team

- Orient project team
- Check on project status with team and/or individual
- Provide feedback to team and/or individual
- Maintain chain of command
- Motivate team
- Develop and/or train staff

### 4. Interfacing with Client and/or User

- Interview to determine needs, project definition
- Meet to discuss design, status, etc.
- Present project information
- Track environment
- Negotiate issues such as changes, procedures, acceptance criteria, staffing, costs
- Respond to needs, demands
- Plan and work towards takeover of system

### 5. Interfacing with the Organization (Beyond Project Team, Client, Users)

- Negotiate for staff, resources
- Provide technical support
- Actively support organizational goals and objectives
- Maintain accountability to IS organization
- Establish effective communication networks
- Enlist timely support from relevant functions within organization

## Project Manager Competencies

Some individuals clearly perform project manager tasks better than others. Superior performers bring to their jobs the right competencies at the right times in the right amounts. Competencies are similar to skills. They are the set of personal attributes that an individual employs while performing his or her job.

Another result of our research was identifying 17 unique competencies that superior project managers use more frequently and with better results than others. These competencies are listed in exhibit 4 and are grouped into four *clusters*.

---

### Exhibit 4: Project Manager Competencies

#### The Problem Solving Cluster

1. Diagnostic Thinking
2. Systematic Thinking
3. Conceptual Thinking
4. Monitoring and Information Gathering

#### The Managerial Identity Cluster

5. Strong Project Manager Identity
6. Self-Confidence
7. Flexibility

#### The Achievement Cluster

8. Concern for Achievement
9. Results Orientation
10. Initiative
11. Business Orientation

#### The Influence Cluster

12. Organizational and Interpersonal Astuteness
13. Skillful Use of Influence Strategies
14. Team Building
15. Developing Others
16. Client/User Orientation
17. Self-Control

---

Different projects require different competencies. Even different phases of the same project require different competencies for effective management. Not surprisingly, we also found that different industries, companies, and organizations prioritize competencies differently. For example, a project in the requirements definition phase will benefit from a manager who displays strength in (1) Diagnostic Thinking, (12) Organizational and Interpersonal Astuteness, and (16) Client/User Orientation competencies. On the other hand, when the same project is heavily into the construction or programming phases, it will be most enhanced by a project manager displaying (5) Strong Project Manager Identity, (9) Results Orientation, and (14) Team Building competencies.

We also developed profiles that help us determine the best fit between project and project manager. We chart the competencies that a job requires and match them with a project manager who possesses those competencies, resulting in a *job/person* profile (Fig. 4). This also helps us identify weak individual competencies that will benefit from additional skills training.

The sequence of events for selecting a project manager—at least for projects of major size—is as follows:

1. Derive several independent evaluations of the competencies or skills most required by the project at hand.

2. Select an individual who appears to best possess those competencies.

3. Obtain the individual's assessment of his or her own competencies as well as the manager's assessments of the individual's competencies.

4. Have the project manager and his or her manager come to an agreement on their respective assessments.

5. Evaluate these competencies against the needs of the project. Provide training, coaching and/or monitoring in any required competency areas.

## Figure 4: Job/Person Competency Profile

1. Transfer the person competency scored from the Person Competency Profile to the designated blank lines underneath grid.
2. Transfer the job competency scores from the Job Competency Profile to the designated blank lines underneath grid.
3. Mark and connect the points on the grid indicating the person competency scores.
4. In a different color pencil or pen, carry out the same procedure for the job competency scores.

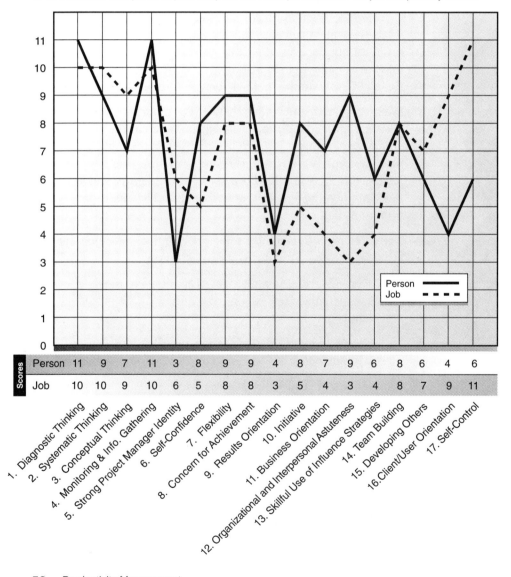

| Scores | | | | | | | | | | | | | | | | | |
|---|---|---|---|---|---|---|---|---|---|---|---|---|---|---|---|---|---|
| Person | 11 | 9 | 7 | 11 | 3 | 8 | 9 | 9 | 4 | 8 | 7 | 9 | 6 | 8 | 6 | 4 | 6 |
| Job | 10 | 10 | 9 | 10 | 6 | 5 | 8 | 8 | 3 | 5 | 4 | 3 | 4 | 8 | 7 | 9 | 11 |

1. Diagnostic Thinking
2. Systematic Thinking
3. Conceptual Thinking
4. Monitoring & Info. Gathering
5. Strong Project Manager Identity
6. Self-Confidence
7. Flexibility
8. Concern for Achievement
9. Results Orientation
10. Initiative
11. Business Orientation
12. Organizational and Interpersonal Astuteness
13. Skillful Use of Influence Strategies
14. Team Building
15. Developing Others
16. Client/User Orientation
17. Self-Control

The project manager profiled in figure 4 would benefit from improving the following competencies in order to prepare for the project: (5) Strong Project Manager Identity, (16) Client/User Orientation and (17) Self-Control.

## Project Management Authority

In determining the roles and responsibilities of the project manager, the subject of his or her **authority** frequently surfaces. Project management authority should be clearly assigned to a single individual by written notice from senior management. Failure to do so makes the job of the project manager much more difficult.

Simple assignment of authority, however, is not enough. An old axiom holds true on this subject: *Authority must be assumed as well as assigned.* If a project manager takes responsibility for actions and activities, he or she will soon have all the authority needed. The six principles of Productivity Management are designed to give a project manager a guide to those areas which he or she should assume responsibility for, thereby gaining appropriate authority.

## Taking Over a Project Already in Progress

In an ideal world, your project management role will be performed on a brand new project. Life isn't always ideal, however, and sometimes you will have to assume management of a project that is already under way. The previous project manager will have been promoted to a new position or removed from the project, leaving you the remains. There are a few steps you should follow before you can pick up where the last manager left off.

- Make sure your project management assignment is formally communicated in writing, especially to any customers and managers of support areas with whom you will interface. Do not accept casual, verbal project management assignment.

- Get a clear definition of what phase of the systems development life cycle the project is in. Make sure that all tasks associated with preceding phases have been accomplished. Don't just take someone's word for it. Verify the delivered products and signed acceptances. Many excellent project managers get into a world of trouble because they take responsibility for tasks that they assumed were already done.

- Review the objectives and plans.

- Review the estimates and the work breakdown structure.

- Check out the job assignments.

Take a close look at what you are getting into. You want the project to be a winning experience for you and for the project team. Make the project your own. If the existing plans are okay, go for it. If not, now is the time to speak up. There is no law that says you have to follow the previous project manager's plans. When you first join a project is the best time to set up a winning arrangement.

## Auditing a Project: Getting Help

Managers within our industry have a tendency not to ask for help. At times this is an admirable trait but not in the management of projects. Do not martyr yourself, silently and stoically watching your project slip into the abyss. There is too much at stake … to you, to your team, to your customers, and to your organization. Your management is there to help you. If they will not or cannot, consult periodicals, books, seminars, consultants, and friends. Don't hesitate to take advantage of all the help you can get. There is no shame in it, especially compared to the potential agony of a failed project.

Keane has a policy of providing a project audit review to any project manager who requests one. The audit is a relatively formal process conducted by a peer or manager who talks to the entire extended team. A day or two is scheduled for the review at a site where the auditor can work uninterrupted.

Arrangements for interviews must be made in advance. The Project Control Book must be fully updated with all current data. All relevant project management and control information must be available. After the project manager orients the auditor, he or she reviews the entire work breakdown structure in detail. All estimates and personnel assignments are evaluated. Project progress on all fronts and for all tasks is reviewed historically. The auditor does a detailed analysis of the project on the basis of the Principles of Productivity Management and shares the results with the project manager and anyone the project manager designates to see them.

Audits are frequently scheduled as tasks integral to the project. They are line item entries on the work breakdown structures and are directly chargeable to the project—as well they should be. Management and the project team should decide the schedule, magnitude, and quantity of these audits at the beginning of the project. As a guide, for a Keane project of more than four persons scheduled to take over six months, we would expect at least one audit. An audit every three of four months would not be unreasonable.

Seven or eight times out of ten, the audit quickly identifies problems and their solutions. This activity can revitalize and streamline a project experiencing problems or midterm lag.

## Chapter Summary: Get the Right People Involved

1. You will never be able to get or keep all the "right" people. The project manager must spend the time getting the people they have "rightly involved."

2. Identify and fully involve all members of the extended team. This will include all major participants from customers, Information Systems, technical support, vendors, operations, etc.

3. Stay attuned to the Project Management Resources Triangle of time, cost/hours, and functionality, and the role it plays in successful project management.

4. The greater role the team members can play in setting project goals, the more successful the project will be.

5. Maslow's "Hierarchy of Needs" can help guide a project manager to maintaining team motivation over the life of a project.

6. The more team members set their own goals, the more successful the project will be for them individually and the greater the likelihood of overall project success.

7. The project team concept remains one of the most powerful techniques for creating sustained effort toward a common goal. The project manager must build and foster this team recognition.

8. Special emphasis should be applied to building the relationship with the project customers and to maintaining their active involvement.

9. The project manager should clearly recognize what his or her job functions and tasks are.

10. Functions and tasks are enhanced by the appropriate use of the right project manager competencies.

11. Do not hesitate to ask for help if the project seems in trouble.

# 3

## Principle Three:
## Estimate the Time and Costs

# Estimate the Time and Costs

For years, we in Information Systems have searched in vain for the key to exact estimating. We have combed ancient scriptures, prayed to divinities, and scaled treacherous, ice-covered mountains to consult cave-dwelling sages. Somewhere out there must lurk the perfect algorithm which, once fed a few discrete variables, gives the precise cost of a proposed project. Alas, we have never found the algorithm. But we have gained enlightenment: the key is that there is no key.

Knowing how much a project will cost comes from experience and effort. Estimating is not—and probably will never be—a solely technical activity. It involves weighing the relative importance of variables, not just plugging them in. It is a management activity and as such is more of an art than a science.

There are two basic reasons that estimating has been a problem for software developers. First, most Information Systems processes do not conform to the basic laws of the physical sciences; we cannot measure a software package's length and width, then calculate the average time it took to develop each inch. Second, we have never really tracked what we do. Many software developers believe that their work is so technically complex and so dependent on individual skill that it cannot be measured.

Both of the above excuses are red herrings. There *are* ways to measure project performance and the industry is finally coming around. It is your responsibility as a project manager to avail yourself of information from past projects for assistance with your estimates and to thoroughly document your process for future project managers.

It is safe to assume that all software development estimates contain a high level of inaccuracy. This will probably be the case for at least another decade or so. By that time, the industry will begin to benefit from the growing practice of monitoring the process of software development. In the interim, close management of the estimating process is required.

# Basics of Estimating

## Why Do We Need Estimates?

If estimates take so much time and effort and are still inaccurate, why bother?

Tracking progress for more accurate estimating in the future is obviously not the only benefit of estimates. Estimates serve to

- Assist in the definition process
- Determine whether there is benefit to pursuing the project
- Establish priorities among projects and activities
- Schedule resources and deliverables within the project
- Track and measure against the project activity
- Ensure that there is enough money to finance the project and to predict cash flows
- Make capital expenditures that may be required to support the project
- Determine annual budgets in anticipation of resource requirements, salaries, facilities, training, and equipment
- Make build-or-buy decisions or consider alternative approaches to meeting the customer's needs.

While estimates may lack something in accuracy, they do at least supply a guideline to follow. Without the plan that comes from the estimate, you will never know if you are making any progress or if you are moving in the right direction. You wouldn't head off on a family vacation with the minivan stuffed full of kids and gear without directions or an estimated arrival time. Starting a project without a decent plan and estimate is similarly foolish.

What an estimate *should not* be used for is a punishment guide. The estimate is a guide for achieving project success, not for concluding that someone is performing poorly. If estimates inspire fear in the project team, morale will be low and the team's future estimates will be artificially padded, making it difficult to track progress. In short, the project—and the organization—will suffer.

## When to Estimate: Early and Often

It almost goes without saying that everybody will complete an estimate at the beginning of a project. The problem is that, for many organizations, that initial estimate is also the final estimate; they never change it. Estimating should not be a onetime affair. At Keane, our policy is to estimate at the beginning of the project; estimate at the end of each phase for the next phase; estimate the project again if there is a major change of scope, of management, of tools, or of procedures; estimate at the end of each reporting period (which is weekly); and estimate again anytime there is concern to warrant it.

An estimate should be the most accurate representation of what is required to complete a project based on the most up-to-date information. As the project progresses, you will inevitably have a clearer idea of what is required, and the estimate should be adjusted accordingly. Estimating should be an ongoing activity over the life of the project. It might be referred to as "reestimating" once the initial estimates have been completed, but it should be done regardless of the name.

## What Is an Estimate?

An estimate—known in the world of systems development as an *estimate to complete* or an *estimate at completion*—is defined as a best guess at how many hours, dollars, people, and machines it will take to complete a project from start to finish. It does not include any change budget or contingency reserves. A figure that includes a change budget or management contingency of any kind would be a *budget to complete* and is different. No estimate should include any hidden pad (a devious concept that will be discussed shortly).

The original estimate from which the project begins is the *baseline* or *performance measurement baseline (PMB).* Based on this performance measurement baseline, you will track progress and evaluate the performance of your project team at the end of the project. The performance measurement baseline does not change over the life of the project without a formally authorized and approved change of scope. (Of course, most projects do change in scope and therefore require adjustment of the PMB.) The baseline upon which you measure performance needs to remain relatively fixed, but the *estimate to complete* will probably change at each activity review.

# Mechanics of Estimating

## Varying Levels of Accuracy in Estimating

A much higher level of accuracy is required to schedule and track resources than to determine annual budgets. The more accurate the estimate needs to be, the more concerted the time and effort spent breaking the job down and estimating smaller pieces must be. This suggests then, that whenever an estimate is requested, you need to make sure that there is a clear, mutual understanding of its purpose and of how accurate it needs to be. You should give no estimate without first asking, "What is the purpose of the estimate and how accurate should it be?"

Generally speaking, there are three estimating stages:

1. An estimate for a *proposal* represents a general or ballpark estimate of the time and cost.

2. An estimate submitted with the *statement of work* will be the final estimate from which approving authorization will be drawn and which will provide the initial performance measurement baseline.

3. An estimate prepared *when the work is assigned* to resources is the estimate submitted by the individual actually doing the work and will become his or her commitment to complete. (Team estimating is discussed below.)

Roughly corresponding to the three estimating stages, there are three levels of confidence in estimating (see figure 5).

An *Order of Magnitude (–25 to +75 percent)* is an approximation, often expressed in a range, made without detailed data. This type of estimate is used during the formative stages of an expenditure program for initial project evaluation. Other terms commonly used to identify an order of magnitude effort are "preliminary," "conceptual," "factored," "quickie," "feasibility," and "SWAG."

A *Budget Estimate (–10 to +25 percent)* is prepared from flow sheets, layouts, and high-level Data Flow Diagrams, and usually represents some level of coarse project breakdown. These estimates are usually established based on some quantitative information and are frequently used to establish funds required, and to obtain approval of the project.

A *Definitive Estimate (–5 to +10 percent)* is prepared from well-defined data, specifications, narratives, and work breakdown structures. These estimates are used for the final project approval and for subsequently tracking performance against plan.

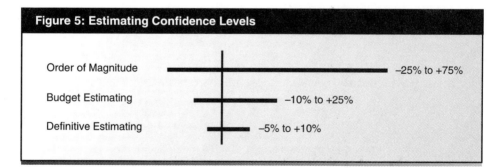

**Figure 5: Estimating Confidence Levels**

Order of Magnitude — –25% to +75%

Budget Estimating — –10% to +25%

Definitive Estimating — –5% to +10%

If a customer asks for a ballpark estimate, that is what you should give. Certainly, we have an obligation to provide an estimate to the best of our ability. And if someone high enough and powerful enough in the organization demands it, we *will* provide that estimate. Where we make the grand mistake is in providing a single, precise number with no context of accuracy. Providing a range estimate will help solve both problems and will be a more accurate reflection of reality.

If a higher level of accuracy is needed, all players must recognize that to define the project, create a work breakdown structure, and determine dependencies and the availability of the required resources will take considerably more time than a ballpark estimate. Even then, the figure is still an estimate: the best guess at what a project will cost. Providing a range estimate may continue to be entirely appropriate. It is only once the project is under way and resources have been assigned that you should switch to a single-figure estimate, which then is the performance measurement baseline.

## The Dangers of Premature Precision

Picture this scenario: Management needs an estimate of costs for a proposed project. They need to know whether the project is worth pursuing. You think the project represents a genuine need. You do some projections and give your estimate: "This job will cost $268,400.55."

Premature precision of this sort is deadly.

Once you have provided that initial—and somehow exact— estimate, the figure becomes carved in a block of granite that you end up wearing around your neck for the remainder of the project. Months later, even though changes of scope have nearly doubled the estimate, the number that people remember is that precise estimate you gave them in the murky past.

Ironically, premature precise estimates are submitted by some of the most experienced people. Having worked on similar projects and feeling confident about their experience, they assume that no problems will arise with the new project and that the costs will be approximately the same as before. This is almost never the case. If a customer needs simply to see whether there is potential profit in a project, an order of magnitude estimate may be adequate. The response to such a request would not be $268,400.55, but a range estimate: $200,000 to 470,000. There is an appropriate time for precise estimates, and it is not at the beginning of a project.

*Avoid premature cost precision.*

## Estimating Techniques

Broadly speaking, there are two distinct estimating approaches: top down and bottom up.

***Top-down*** estimating is when you evaluate several major influences on the size of the project and draw relatively quick conclusions from them. You might, for example, look only at inputs, outputs and integrating entities and make your estimates based on how long those activities might take. Top-down estimates are also frequently done from various parametrics and cost estimating relationships.

*Bottom-up* estimating refers to breaking the job down into pieces and estimating each piece. The estimates are added up to provide a more detailed overall estimate.

Within the two broad categories of top-down and bottom-up estimating there are dozens of individualized techniques, most of which can be used for both estimating methods. There is a time, place, and advantage for each. Below is a sample list of some of those techniques:

- COCOMO
- Function Point Analysis
- Feature Point Analysis
- Work Distribution Models
- Delphi Techniques
- Putnam distribution (PERT)
- Analogous
- Cost Estimating Relationships
- Matrix

Theoretically, you could use a few different estimating techniques on one project since you might find a technique appropriate for one phase but not another. In order for an estimating technique to be effective on the whole project, it must be (1) workable, (2) logical, (3) consistent, and (4) self-improving, four concepts explained below.

*Workable* means that an estimating technique can be applied to all or most of the activities being performed in a project. That is to say, it will work equally well for estimating programming tasks as for analysis, design, interviewing, testing, etc. Some estimating techniques are appropriate only for certain tasks.

The estimating technique should be *logical*, meaning it should be logically and easily understood so that even a novice to the business can follow how to use it. Some estimating procedures work relatively well, but they are so complex in their use that they are better avoided. If greater complexity produced superior results, you would not hear the admonition, "Keep it simple, stupid" (KISS) so often. Generally, the simpler the technique, the better its performance.

An estimating technique should be *consistent* in its application and use. Can it be applied in a consistent fashion across a broad spectrum of activities and be consistently applied from one project to the next? If you want to become adept at using a tool, you have to keep using that same tool over some period of time. Artisans don't hone their skills by changing tools every week. But in information technology, we seem to feel the need for a new tool for every project. Whether it is a programming language, a word processor, project management software, or an estimating technique, you should use a single tool long enough to become skilled in its use.

Lastly, an estimating technique should be *self-improving*. That is to say, it should allow the estimator to get better at its use through simple modification of certain variables. Based on a review of previous projects, you may find that your initial set of variables will require adjustment. The estimating technique should support that adjustment.

## The Continuing Role of Work Breakdown Structures

In Chapter 1, the work breakdown structure was introduced to help define the job in detail by breaking it into tasks. Estimating reaps similar benefits from job breakdown. The primary advantage to task-by-task estimating is that individual tasks can be more easily and accurately estimated than can the project as a whole. Even if estimates for individual tasks are off by a large percentage, the error will be small in the context of the entire project, and such errors may cancel each other out in the balance. Breaking the job down also ensures that the estimator has a good understanding of the project, thereby eliminating semi-informed guessing.

Breaking the job down into its component parts for estimating is related to the principle of Chapter 4, "Break the Job Down Using the 80-Hour Rule," where the job is broken down into tasks of not more than 80 hours' duration. At the initial stages of a project, however, you will probably lack the sufficient analysis to break the entire project into tasks of 80 hours or less. You can go only as far as the available information and time will allow.

For all but the most accurate estimates, breaking the job down involves first identifying the major products to be developed within the project. Each of these products is then segmented into smaller products. The process continues until the lowest appropriate deliverable product or segment of a product is reached. The more complete the up-front analysis, the more detailed the breakdown segments, and consequently, the more accurate the estimate.

## Developing Team Member Estimating Skills

As project manager, you must require and foster the development of estimating skills within the project team. One simple fact about management is that *the project manager will never be any better than his or her team.* You obviously want to have the very best team possible, and a significant step toward creating the best team possible is to get them to be the best estimators possible.

Every week, you will want the team to provide a revised estimate-to-complete for their respective tasks. Your success at knowing the true status of the project and where to make any necessary adjustments will depend on the accuracy of the team's estimates. Encourage them to estimate and reestimate continually. Make sure that they have the same tools and techniques that are available to you. You will benefit and so will they.

## Validating the Estimate

Breaking a job down and estimating each of its components independently is essential for accuracy. Also indispensable is analyzing that task-by-task estimate from a broader perspective—comparing a bottom-up with a top-down estimate of some sort. This comparison can provide excellent balance. A project manager preparing a task-by-task estimate may be overly concerned with the myriad details of the project and overlook broader issues. A more general approach would provide the opportunity to consider the big picture. In addition, when many members of the project team are doing task-by-task estimates there are occasionally duplications of functions which a top-down estimate may detect.

At Keane, we also validate large and/or high-impact projects through secondary estimates. Our approach is somewhat akin to a standard Wide-Band Delphi technique, in which we seek three separate estimates and incorporate some median or averaging procedures. We provide each estimator or estimating group with the same specifications. They independently estimate the project, and we then review the estimates collectively, each group sharing their opinions and experience with the others. Based on this shared information, we arrive at a representative estimate with built-in validation.

## Work Distribution Models

A *Work Distribution Model* is a general guide that breaks a project down into its phases and assigns a "percentage-of-whole" amount to each. (The following example represents a hypothetical organization; these percentage distributions vary widely depending on the organization.) You might, for example, find that the phases of your organization's projects usually consume the percentages of the whole project depicted in figure 6.

Using the Work Distribution Model as a guide, you examine your estimates for the project you are working on. Let's assume we have spent $10,000 on the system concept formation phase and $25,000 for the business systems analysis

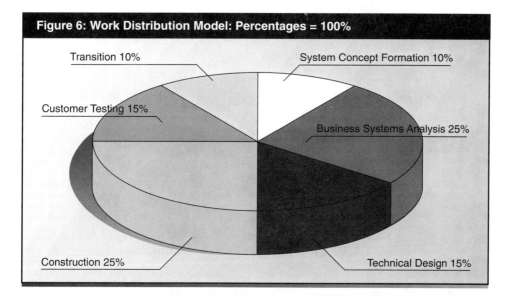

Figure 6: Work Distribution Model: Percentages = 100%

Transition 10%
System Concept Formation 10%
Customer Testing 15%
Business Systems Analysis 25%
Construction 25%
Technical Design 15%

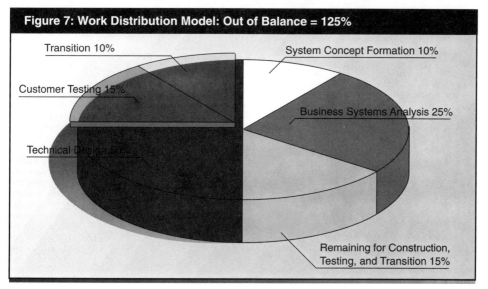

Figure 7: Work Distribution Model: Out of Balance = 125%

Transition 10%
System Concept Formation 10%
Customer Testing 15%
Business Systems Analysis 25%
Technical Design 50%
Remaining for Construction, Testing, and Transition 15%

phase, but our estimate for technical design is $50,000. The ratio of the cost factors in this situation (see figure 7) is sorely out of balance and deserves scrutiny. It may be correct, but we are aware that something *may* be wrong. Perhaps we did not spend adequate time in system concept formation or business systems analysis or both. Maybe we are drifting beyond our scope in technical design. Maybe everything is okay, but we have been alerted, and perhaps it is worth another look.

In order for a Work Distribution Model to be an effective estimating tool, it is essential that each organization develop its own ratios by analyzing its previous projects, taking into account variables such as project environment, experience of team members, language, hardware, and software. Such an analysis is impossible unless you keep records of all time spent on each project. This tracking is exactly what the automated project modeling and planning tools have done, and it is the technique they use to estimate projects. Most of them have a base of hundreds of thousands or even millions of hours of tracked projects from a multitude of different organizations.

If you continue to track projects in sufficient detail over a long enough period of time, you will be able to break the phases down and assign standard percentages to each activity. (Recall that the basic hierarchy for a project's work breakdown structure is *project, phase, activity, task,* and *subtask.*) Eventually, even tasks within activities will assume a standard percentage distribution, but it may take thousands of tracked project hours to get to such accurate levels.

The Work Distribution Model, also referred to as ***balance of cost factors***, is a helpful tool in reviewing a project estimate, but should not be used for the actual estimate. It is a top-down technique and is too broad for actual estimating. It does, however, flag potential problem areas when used as a comparison guide.

## Risk Analysis and Mitigation

One way to approach a project realistically is to consider risks. Evaluating the risks should be an inherent part of estimating— the risk that the project will take longer, cost more, or require more effort than planned. The existence of risk is the reason an estimate is necessary in the first place; without it, you would simply inform the customer of the time and cost required for a project and execute it to the hour and to the dime. But every project possesses multiple variables, and when supplying an estimate, you should also supply a risk factor.

By risk, we do not mean uncertainty. *Uncertainty* implies only that an event may or may not occur. *Risk* implies knowledge of the probability of an event occurring. One is manageable, the other is not.

One fall morning, a facility of ours shut down as a result of snakes moving into an underground electrical junction box, thinking they had found a comfortable winter hibernation spot. Their squirming caused an electrical short and small explosion that brought down the entire communication linkage.

There is no way that we could have been aware of the potential of this snake situation, and it therefore falls in the category of uncertainty. Snake interference is not a variable considered in the management of a project. If, however, we view the snakes from the standpoint of "Might our communications facilities go down during the course of this project?" then we have risk. We can make a statistical evaluation of how likely *some* unforeseen event is and estimate the dollar and time impact of that occurrence.

We know, for example, that during any given 30-day period, there is a 40% likelihood that the communication facilities at the site in question will be interrupted by *something,* and that the interruption will average about four hours. If we plan to have five programmers working on a project over six months, we can calculate the probability and cost of the interruption, and our estimates can reflect that risk.

Risk can be difficult to identify and quantify. Nevertheless, by maintaining records of all projects, an organization can consult histories of projects to estimate associated risks. Each organization should identify those factors that can have a significant impact on an estimate, and through organizational experience develop quantitative values for each. These quantitative values should identify the probability of the occurrence and its impact in dollars or hours. At Keane, this is a part of our "living laboratory" approach to project management, and we find that it contributes significantly to estimating accuracy.

All members of the extended project team should, at some point, participate in a session devoted to risk identification, assessment, and mitigation. All potential elements of risk should be identified, as should the likelihood of their occurrence and the potential impact on the project. Techniques for minimizing those risks should then be determined and implemented. A few of the more readily identifiable risk items are noted below. Successful risk analysis, however, will focus on the specific project at hand to determine risks unique to it.

- Volatility of requirements: are the customer's requirements well defined or loose and unstructured?
- Size and complexity of the project
- Complexity of the technology
- Inexperience of the project manager, development team, and/or customer with the application, language, other associated software packages, and hardware (particularly communication)
- Organizational climate
- Resource availability
- Governmental regulations
- Weather and seasons

A common problem is, instead of applying risk analysis to a project, a project team will simply state assumptions:

- We will have a full staff complement of eight by April 15.

- The servers and communication lines will be installed by June 30.

- The customers will sign off on delivered items within four working days.

These assumptions are great, but what if they don't happen? Stating an assumption does not take the situation far enough. If you can assume or anticipate an event, then you should be able to weigh the consequences. That is risk analysis. The basis for an assumption then becomes a criterion for acceptance. If it is not met during system design, it is a change and should be managed accordingly.

If you do not have a full complement of staff by April 15, the likelihood of completing the project on schedule will be reduced by 12% each day until it is reached. Now you can apply a time and dollar value. The 12% is based on historical perspective, current staffing problems, gut feel, or whatever influences on staff issues exist.

Eventually, you and the project team should be able to reach a point where you can give some assessment of the accuracy of your estimates. Based on the summed probability and impact of risks, you might suggest, for example, that an estimate is assessed to be within a 90% level of accuracy. One could also address the accuracy of estimates through standard deviation. However it is expressed, risk should be considered a major element of project estimating.

Individual elements of risk can accumulate and if risk analysis yields a high probability for project failure, the project should not be undertaken until circumstances change. It takes pretty gutsy (read: foolish) management to proceed when the summed probability of failure is above 50%. Many will stop well below that figure.

## Phase Review and Estimate Refinement

Although the general estimate for the entire project can serve as a useful starting point, the most accurate and reliable estimate is the one for the next phase to be worked on. Each phase should be estimated prior to being authorized. During the execution of a phase, the parameters and requirements for the next phase are established, and enough information becomes available to accurately estimate that next phase. As each phase is more accurately estimated, the overall estimate for the entire project can be reviewed and refined.

Since the activity of estimating each phase and refining the overall estimate is an integral part of the development process, the estimating task should be included in the definition and project plan. This facilitates ongoing, formal reevaluation of the project. If the project plan clearly states that a review of the estimate will be made at the completion of each phase, all concerned parties are made aware that the estimate is subject to refinement as the details of the project become more defined.

As each new estimate is submitted, the customer can reevaluate the project to check that it remains within an acceptable cost/benefit range. If it is not acceptable, the customer weighs alternatives: should they scale down the scope of the project? increase the budget? abandon the project? Admittedly, these alternatives can be unpleasant to consider when time, money, and effort have already been expended, but it is better to consider them before expenditures of even more time and money mount beyond control.

The virtue of reestimating does not relieve the manager of time and cost constraints that may exist on a project. If a date simply must be met, or there is an absolute cap on expenditures, that mandate must be followed. If a refined estimate indicates the need to exceed the set limit for time or money, other factors must change to keep the project in line. Keep the time-cost-functionality triangle in mind (figure 2).

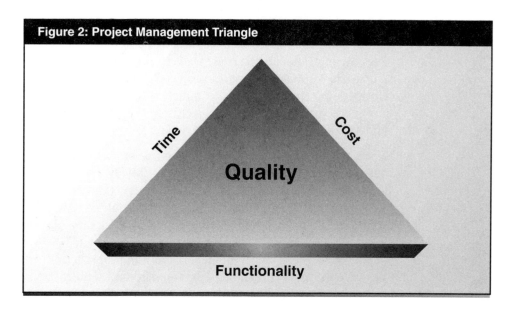

**Figure 2: Project Management Triangle**

Time

Cost

Quality

Functionality

Perhaps you cut functionality or bring on more people. If one side of the triangle changes, something must happen to one or both of the remaining sides.

## Building Experience with Post-Project Reviews

Ultimately, the most important ingredient in estimating is *experience*—the experience of the individual doing the estimating and of the Information Systems staff. Only when the estimates and actuals of all projects are compared can estimating accuracy be maximized and the full value be gained from each project. Knowing what projects cost and knowing what percentage of past projects were devoted to design, coding, testing, etc., provides invaluable input for estimating subsequent projects. In the project review, judgments should be made as to why estimates were or were not achieved while details are still fresh in the minds of the participants. Reviews also help the organization determine how well it performed on different aspects of project development: What are the effects of unscheduled activities on the organization's estimates? How do you sufficiently provide for unforeseens in the future? Is the organization more accurate in estimating coding than design ... or testing ... or documentation? Does the organization fall apart when estimating complex projects? All of this information is available at the completion of a project and can have predictive value if each project is subjected to a well-run and well-documented post-project review.

Such a valuable activity, however, seems to be rarely done. Most organizations simply do not plan for review as a part of the project. Project team members are reassigned immediately leaving no time for an effective post-project analysis. Each project should have as a line item entry in its work breakdown structure a task called "quality review," "project audit," "postmortem" or whatever nomenclature is appropriate for your organization. This should be a standard task with costs attributable to the project itself with a scheduled time frame, deliverable products, and assigned responsibility.

Organizations that do budget for reviews find they more than pay for themselves by increasing estimating accuracy, thereby generating more successful projects. Improved accuracy is often accomplished in as few as three or four projects and their associated reviews.

## Additional Estimating Considerations

### The Pad

The second most insidious problem in the estimating process, behind failure to measure progress, is the pad. Of course, the two problems are related: if we had been measuring all along, we would not feel the need for a padded estimate in the first place.

A pad is an unspecified amount of money or hours scattered secretly and arbitrarily throughout a project's tasks and activities. Pads attempt to cover anything from a minor report change to a nuclear meltdown. Many a project manager has hunched furtively over project plans, secretly scattering about bits of time and dollars, thinking, "My boss will never find them this time, and we'll finally be under budget." The problem with a pad is that no one knows how much it is, where it is, or what it is supposed to be used for—usually, not even the project manager who put it there. We can effectively manage only that which is visible and known. We cannot, therefore, expect something like an invisible pad to be manageable.

Eliminating the pad does not mean that you cannot plan for variables and unknowns. Aboveboard methods of preparing for possible runover fall into the category of *What a pad is not:*

- A pad *is not* a 15% increase added across the board to all programming tasks because the team would be working in an unfamiliar programming language.

- A pad *is not* a single line item of the work breakdown structure titled something like "Reserve for contingency," "Management reserve," "Money to deal with a difficult customer," "Change of scope budget," or even "Pad." (Most of these items would be handled through the formal Change of Scope procedures discussed in Chapter 5, "Establish a Change Procedure.")

- A pad *is not* a task titled "Probable integration testing foul-ups."

The difference between the above items and the evil pad is that the acceptable items are identified by name and by amount. You can track their use, know how much is left, and manage accordingly. At the end of the project you can determine whether the buffer was enough and do better the next time. By avoiding the pad, you avoid artificially inflating those activities that contain the pad. At the end of the project, your numbers will be honest and helpful for the next estimate you prepare.

## Common Leave-Outs

Estimates made in haste or by inexperienced personnel often focus only on the technical issues and tend to omit important business functions such as project management, documentation, training, and personnel turnover. This will come back to haunt you: it isn't the tasks you planned for that cause you the most pain, it's the things you never planned for at all.

A checklist is useful in ensuring that all cost factors have been included. Each organization should develop one for estimating. Some commonly omitted time and cost elements are identified below.

*Project Management.* All projects require some level of project management, and the time required for this activity must be included in the estimate. At Keane, our experience suggests that project management accounts for 10% to 20% of the overall budget, depending on the nature of the project. Currently, we appear to be running at about 12% to 15%. Conversions, for example, where activities are often repeated, generally require less management than new development. High-risk projects require strong, effective management and therefore should have a larger percentage of the budget devoted to project management. Each organization should maintain records to determine its own management costs.

*Turnover.* Turnover is particularly important on large projects. It creates real time and money costs. New personnel must become familiar with the project, learn the hardware and software, and develop the appropriate team relationships that will permit effective communication. If turnover is likely to involve hiring new people, hiring costs must also be considered.

*Salary Changes.* Salary changes over the life of lengthy projects must be considered within the cost estimates. Generally, they contribute to increased project costs, and while simple to estimate they are often forgotten in the estimating process.

*Experience and Ability of Team Personnel.* Capable, experienced people usually more than compensate for their higher pay, but they will be expecting interesting and challenging assignments. Generally speaking, one should use the least expensive resources that can do the job well.

## Optimism

The unbounded optimism so frequently present in the software development industry can occasionally have a negative effect, particularly in estimating. It sometimes leads project managers to assume that the next project will be perfect . . . even though none of the previous eleven were. They imagine that the programs will contain only a couple of small bugs, that testing will go smoothly, and that errors will be few. This time the project team will all get along in perfect harmony, and the customers will be simply delighted with everything. Optimism and short memories can produce some unrealistic estimates. When estimating projects, it is best to use a pragmatic, realistic approach.

## Put *Everything* in Writing

Assumptions can significantly affect time and cost throughout the project. Assumptions are usually verbal agreements, and verbal agreements can be fleeting. A general rule at Keane is that if it isn't in writing, it didn't happen. Responsibilities specified in writing are far more likely to be heeded than those agreed to verbally. When everything is explicitly addressed in writing, you avoid the conflicts that arise from unshared assumptions and from circumstances that change without notice.

## The Use of Automated Tools in the Estimating Process

The ever-burgeoning software market for project management is continuously trying to help improve the estimating process. The market's contributions are occurring on five main fronts:

1. The development of detailed system and project life cycles has resulted in an increasing pool of approaches to project management.

2. Management software provides estimates for tasks based on the accumulation of thousands (even millions) of hours of previous project experience.

3. There is software that provides you with the ability to adapt and continually modify information based on your own organization's history so estimates are more relevant to your project histories.

4. The software market has developed better review and analysis techniques that improve your ability to estimate completions and identify problems.

5. The software provides data repositories that allow you to retain project information and readily access it for analysis and forecasting.

Keane uses the automated estimating tools principally for initial proposal preparation and to do validation estimates of our detailed bottom-up estimates. Proposals that used to take eight to twelve hours can now be completed in three or four. We may also use estimating tools to do our initial planning for approved projects. If we believe the project is similar enough to the automated work breakdown structures, we will accept the automatically generated project as a basis to start planning.

Learning to use these tools effectively requires time. It is not unusual for an individual to spend 60 hours of training and practice to become relatively proficient with the use of automated tools. It is probably not appropriate to expect everyone in the organization to become familiar with their use. Instead, selected individuals should be trained in the software to permit adequate organizational coverage. Once in place, the automated estimating tools can offer significant productivity gains in preparing proposals and implementing projects. They will also provide a valuable secondary source for validating estimates.

**Exhibit 5: Estimating Checklist**

- Identify the purpose of the estimate and what level of accuracy is required. This is a good time to consider the three levels of accuracy: Order of Magnitude, Budget, and Definitive.
- Break the job down to the appropriate level of detail.
- Estimate each task separately and apply effort hours.
- If needed, assign hourly rates and extend.
- Identify, evaluate, and control all risks.
- Establish a summary total of detailed task estimates.
- Include all other cost factors (project management, training, etc.).
- Establish the final estimate.
- Validate the estimate.
- Provide only a range estimate for all general and overall estimates.
- Determine final Performance Measurement Baseline.
- Add contingency reserve or change budget.
- Identify the final Budget at Completion.
- Clearly identify in writing all assumptions and constraints on which the estimate is based.
- Estimate and plan a post-project review.
- Reestimate throughout the project.

# Chapter Summary: Estimate the Time and Costs

1. Accurate estimates will continue to be difficult to achieve until we start measuring what we do.

2. Project managers must identify and understand why they are providing estimates for their organization. For what purposes will they be used?

3. Estimates should be provided at many points throughout the life of a project, not just at the beginning. Reestimating should occur at every reporting period.

4. An estimate is a best guess of the hours, dollars, or time to complete a project, phase, activity, or task within the project.

5. An estimate to complete refers to how long it will take to complete a defined activity. A Budget at Completion includes an estimate to complete plus a budget for change. A Performance Management/Measurement Baseline (PMB) identifies a relatively fixed estimate of hours or dollars for any calendar point over the life of the project.

6. Increased accuracy of estimates demands more time in defining tasks. When asked for an estimate, determine the purpose of the estimate and how accurate you must be.

7. Estimating accuracy levels of confidence vary from a low level, which is termed an "Order of Magnitude," through "Budgetary," to the highest level, termed "Definitive."

8. Avoid premature precision. Do not provide estimates until you know what you are estimating and under what demands.

9. Estimates are categorized as either top-down (broad, quick estimates usually derived from some sort of relational parameters) or bottom-up (derived from a more detailed task-by-task definition).

10. Estimating techniques should be workable, logical, consistent and self-improving.

11. The work breakdown structure derived from the systems development life cycles will be a guide in determining what to estimate.

12. Everybody on the team should participate in reestimating their assignments every week.

13. Using a Work Distribution Model is a top-down technique that helps validate a bottom-up estimate.

14. Risk analysis is an integral part of the estimating process that will identify probability and consequence to activities within the project. Risk should be measured and managed.

15. Project estimates should be closely reviewed and compared at the completion of the project in order to improve estimating accuracy.

16. Estimates should reflect only the best guess at the actual effort involved and should not include a randomly dispersed pad.

17. Some activities such as project management are best estimated as a percent of the total technical effort.

18. There are many automated tools that will help model and estimate the project or parts of the project.

# 4

## Principle Four:
## Break the Job Down Using the 80-Hour Rule

# Break the Job Down Using the 80-Hour Rule

One of the main reasons for developing the Principles of Productivity Management was to create some technique to better measure project status and to eliminate the 90% Done Syndrome discussed in Chapter 1, in which the final 10% of the project tends to take as long as the first 90%. In the early years of software development (and even well into recent years), project teams lacked the models to accurately track and report project status. At Keane, we set out to develop a technique that would enable us to tie *efforts* with *results:* to compare the time, money, and work put into a project with the products that emerged. The 80-Hour Rule is that technique, and it may be the single most powerful concept of the Principles of Productivity Management.

## The 80-Hour Rule

### The 80-Hour Rule Defined

The 80-Hour Rule stipulates that you break a project into tasks of 80 hours or less, each of which must result in a tangible product or deliverable. No matter what is included in a task, no more than two weeks of *elapsed time* should be required to complete it. Under this structure, a task will often require fewer than 80 hours but should never require more. Since each task will produce a deliverable, at no time will more than 80 hours pass without work being produced and formally monitored. Even on very large projects, there is no activity or event that cannot be broken down into tasks of 80 hours or less.

Use of the 80-Hour Rule overcomes the problems caused by subjective reporting, because reporting on progress is limited to an objective, binary mode: each task is either done or not done. Opinions are not involved. "90% done" is not an option. In addition to this primary advantage of providing tangible tracking and reporting, the 80-Hour Rule also provides a basis for detailed estimating, planning, work assignment, and performance measurement.

Any phase of the development process will usually contain obvious deliverable products, some of which will already be achievable within two elapsed weeks. Products that will take longer than two weeks to complete must be broken down further into tasks that can be delivered by one person in 80 hours or less.

Imagine, for example, that you are developing program specifications. One set of these specifications is the one that defines the input files and transactions that we will refer to as INPUTS. Applying the 80-Hour Rule, you first ask, "Will the preparation of program specs for INPUTS take 80 hours or less of elapsed time for one person to prepare?" If the answer is yes, what *tangible* product(s) will you supply upon completion for evaluation? That is your deliverable product.

If preparing INPUTS specs will take more than 80 hours, as in exhibit 6, you break the job down into smaller tasks. The category INPUTS might, for instance, be broken down further into *types* of inputs:

- Inquiry account inputs
- Maintenance account inputs
- Update account inputs

You then ask the same questions for each of these smaller items. "Can we complete the specs for the *Inquiry account inputs* in 80 hours or less, and what will be the deliverable product(s)?" Breakdown continues until no task requires more than 80 hours for one person to complete.

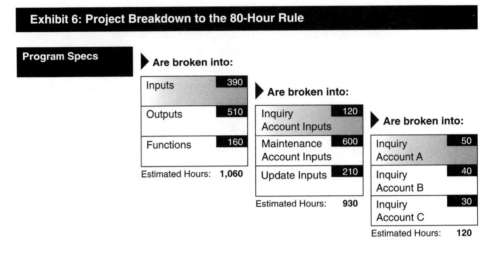

**Exhibit 6: Project Breakdown to the 80-Hour Rule**

**Program Specs**

▶ **Are broken into:**

| Inputs | 390 |
|---|---|
| Outputs | 510 |
| Functions | 160 |

Estimated Hours: **1,060**

▶ **Are broken into:**

| Inquiry Account Inputs | 120 |
|---|---|
| Maintenance Account Inputs | 600 |
| Update Inputs | 210 |

Estimated Hours: **930**

▶ **Are broken into:**

| Inquiry Account A | 50 |
|---|---|
| Inquiry Account B | 40 |
| Inquiry Account C | 30 |

Estimated Hours: **120**

On large projects, this process becomes quite extensive and must be carefully documented. The 80-Hour Rule has been fully and appropriately applied to a project when the following criteria are met:

1. Each task can be done by one person in two elapsed weeks or less.

2. Each task produces a tangible deliverable.

3. Each task can be measured in binary form as done or not done.

Breaking a project down into components requires perseverance and a firm understanding of the application being developed. Once the breakdown is complete, however, even formidably large projects become clear and manageable. This concept is also known as *short interval scheduling* in other industries. Applying the 80-Hour Rule gives you a precise understanding of all tasks to be performed and of what sequence they should be performed in.

## Creating Deliverable Products

One of the most important steps of the 80-Hour Rule is recognizing and/or creating **deliverable products.** Measuring progress is easiest when you use tangible markers, and the best markers in software development are deliverable products.

Using the 80-Hour Rule, we focus on deliverable products in order to avoid entanglements with unreality. A deliverable product is something we can see. A deliverable product is something we can hold in our hands. A deliverable product exists and is tangible. It is real.

Following this precept of the 80-Hour Rule means fully recognizing that anything and everything you do on a project should be translated into a tangible product. For example, to deliver "a program design" is a vague way of considering a task. The task becomes a tangible one, however, if you identify a program design as consisting of the following deliverable products:

1. A written, descriptive narrative;

2. A process flowchart;

3. At least two levels of business process dataflow diagrams;

4. A written preliminary unit test plan.

You can evaluate any one of the real items above and say, "Yes, approved," or "No, it's not quite right. Change it here and here."

Identifying a deliverable product for every single task may be difficult to do in the beginning. It may mean that you have to become more disciplined and imaginative to think in terms of tangible products than you have been in the past. But the results will be worth the effort in your ability to assign work and to mark progress on a project.

## Measuring Productivity

Does a 40-hour workweek really mean 40 hours of work?

The answer, of course, is no, except with a computer—and even then, inevitable downtime prevents such productivity. One hundred percent productivity is simply an unrealistic expectation. Nevertheless, some organizations insist on scheduling projects as if it were possible. Training, nonproject administrative tasks, vacation, holidays, and sick days all prevent people from actively working on a project with 100% productivity.

At 40 hours per week and 52 weeks, there are 2,080 hours a person could work in a year. After monitoring productivity at Keane for many years, we know that the most we can expect from people on a 40-hour week is 1,664 hours per year. On the average, 416 hours will be spent on "nonproductive" or "nonproject" activities. If we were to schedule projects based on the assumption that everyone would be productive for 2,080 hours, people would have to work an extra 416 hours a year in order to compensate for training, vacations, holidays, illness, etc. Not a very fair deal, and certainly a terrible way to schedule a project. And when problems occur—and they will—there would be no leeway to work with. Scheduling 40 hours of actual work per week essentially builds about 25% overtime into the project. Getting 1,664 productive hours a year from your people may sound low, but a productivity level of 80% (1,664/2,080 = 80%) is actually pretty good. Not many organizations do much better, and some don't do nearly as well.

No matter what your organization's productivity level is, you must identify it so you can meaningfully schedule people and project completion dates around it. The pure, unpadded *effort-hours* that you estimated for the project in Chapter 3 can then be converted to *elapsed time* in order to create a realistic schedule for the project.

The distinction between effort-hours and elapsed time is an important one. Effort-hours refers to how many hours of actual work it will take to perform a task or group of tasks. Elapsed time is "calendar time": how much calendar time will be required to complete those effort-hours? Productivity is the ratio of effort-hours to elapsed time.

Nonproductive time is only that time that can be clearly identified and measured. Time closeted in a bathroom stall reading the sports or fashion pages does not count. Meetings and general administration count as nonproductive time if (1) they are not charged to a project, (2) they can be measured, (3) they occur with some level of regularity over the course of a year, and (4) they apply to just about everyone.

When you start tracking productivity, you should measure it at least on a monthly basis. You may be surprised at how it varies during the course of a year. Keane's productivity will run at about 67% between Thanksgiving and New Year's Day but may be as high as 93% in February, March, and April. If there is one thing this information taught us, it is that the end of the year is the very worst time to try to crunch a project through to a finish. The project is more likely to be successful if scheduled to complete at the end of April.

Once you know your organization's or department's productivity rate, you will be able to schedule projects with much greater accuracy. If your productivity rate is 80%, you schedule projects based on a 32-hour workweek. If it is 70%, you schedule 28-hour workweeks. Failure to plan with productivity estimates is casting a blind eye to reality. If you want to strive for a higher level of performance or crash a project, this is not the best place to do it.

Determining actual productivity for your organization will assist in both estimating more accurately and in breaking a job into tasks. Eighty percent productivity does not mean that no one will ever do 40 hours of actual work per week. Indeed, when scheduling their own tasks, team members will often plan to do just that. The overall project, however, should be initially planned using the realistic productivity percentage.

In order to convert actual effort-hours from the estimate into an elapsed time schedule, you use a ***productivity factor***. A productivity factor is determined by taking the reciprocal of the productivity percentage (in this case: $1/.80 = 1.25$). To convert an effort-hours estimate to elapsed time, multiply it by the productivity factor. If, for example, you have estimated that a software program will take 400 hours of effort to write, you multiply 400 (effort-hours) by 1.25 (productivity factor) and come up with elapsed time: 500 hours. In other words, one person working on this activity will need about 500 elapsed hours to complete it. Divide that time by the 40 elapsed hours in a week (or 37.5, or whatever is normal for your organization), and instead of scheduling the task to be completed in 10 weeks, you schedule for 12.5 weeks, which is the more accurate reflection of reality.

## Project Plans

Job breakdown using the 80-Hour Rule is expressed through various project plans and forms. Which forms you use will depend on the automated software, if any, you are running. At Keane, we like to see at least the following forms to outline job breakdown:

- A Gantt chart that shows all tasks in as near a logical sequence as possible, with start and finish times indicated with a bar and in a weekly schedule or a monthly schedule (exhibit 7).

- The same Gantt chart or a similar one that includes estimated hours per week or per month (exhibit 8).

- A form, such as the Weekly Progress Report, for team members to report narratively on work progress.

- A timesheet (exhibit 9) that identifies individual team member assignments and allows people to report effort-hours expended and tasks completed on a weekly basis.

| Name | Est. Hrs. | Res. List | Jul | Aug | Sep | Oct | Nov | Dec | Jan | Feb |
|---|---|---|---|---|---|---|---|---|---|---|

## Business System Analysis

**Project Management**

| Develop Project Plan/Schedule | 32 | PM |
| Manage the Project | 300 | PM |

**Prepare Diagrams**

| Develop the Data Model | 240 | BA CB |
| Develop the Process Model | 292 | BA CB |

**Generate Functional/Data Reqmnts.**

| Write the Primitive Process Specifications | 450 | BA CB CT |
| Generate the Data Dictionary | 260 | CT |
| Reconcile the Process and Data Models | 168 | BA CT CB |

**Generate Performance Reqmnts.**

| Estimate Performance Requirements | 160 | CB BA CT |
| Update the Data Model | 96 | BA CB CT |

**Produce User Reqmnts. Document**

| Gather System Specifications | 276 | BA CB CT |
| Distribute the Draft Specifications | 32 | BA CT |

**Assess Implementation Reqmnts.**

| Assess Technical Issues | 96 | PM BA C |
| Determine Design Approach | 64 | PM BA C |

**User Review of Requirements**

| Prepare for User Reviews | 96 | BA PM C |
| Conduct User Reviews | 112 | BA CM C |

**Decide Changes & Impl. Strategy**

| Accept User Changes | 128 | PM BA C |
| Document Sponsor Decisions | 32 | BA CB |

**Plan Technical Design Phase**

| Develop the Technical Design Plan | 140 | PM BA |
| BSA Complete | | |

## Techncial Design

| SUMMARY Technical Design | 1,800 | TEAM |

## Construction

| SUMMARY Construction | 3,000 | TEAM |

## User Testing

| SUMMARY User Testing | 1,800 | TEAM |

## Transition

| SUMMARY Transition | 1,200 | |
| Totals | 10,774 | |

| Name | Est. Hrs. | Res. List | Jul | Aug | Sep | Oct | Nov | Dec | Jan | Feb |
|---|---|---|---|---|---|---|---|---|---|---|
| Project Manager | 8.0 | PM | 223 | 108 | 93 | 5 | 35 | | | |
| Business Analyst | 8.0 | BA | 582 | 132 | 104 | 86 | 90 | | | |
| Customer Business Expert | 8.0 | CB | 372 | 82 | 12 | 58 | 90 | | | |
| Consultants - Technical | 8.0 | CT | 314 | 182 | 94 | 161 | 72 | | | |
| Customer Manager | 8.0 | CM | 32 | 0 | 0 | 0 | 16 | | | |
| Customer Users | 8.0 | CU | | | | | 32 | | | |
| TEAM | 8.0 | TEAM | | | | | | | | |
| Totals | | | 1,523 | 504 | 303 | 310 | 335 | | | |

## Exhibit 8: Gantt Chart - Numeric Format

| B.E.P.S. Task Name | Task Dura. | Res. Abb. | Total Est. | Jul | Aug | Sep | Oct | Nov | Dec | Jan | Feb |
|---|---|---|---|---|---|---|---|---|---|---|---|
| **Business System Analysis** | | | | | | | | | | | |
| **Project Management** | | | | | | | | | | | |
| Develop Project Plan/Schedule | 4 | PM | 32 | 32 | | | | | | | |
| Manage the Project | 64 | PM | 300 | 99 | 108 | 93 | | | | | |
| **Prepare Diagrams** | | | | | | | | | | | |
| Develop the Data Model | 15 | BA | 120 | 120 | | | | | | | |
| | | CB | 120 | 120 | | | | | | | |
| Develop the Process Model | 23 | BA | 180 | 48 | 132 | | | | | | |
| | | CB | 112 | 30 | 82 | | | | | | |
| **Generate Functional/Data Reqmnts.** | | | | | | | | | | | |
| Write the Primitive Process Specifications | 19 | BA | 150 | 150 | | | | | | | |
| | | CB | 150 | 150 | | | | | | | |
| | | CT | 150 | 150 | | | | | | | |
| Generate the Data Dictionary | 33 | CT | 260 | 16 | 182 | 63 | | | | | |
| Reconcile the Process and Data Models | 15 | BA | 120 | | | 104 | 16 | | | | |
| | | CT | 36 | | | 31 | 5 | | | | |
| | | CB | 12 | | | 12 | 0 | | | | |
| **Generate Performance Reqmnts.** | | | | | | | | | | | |
| Estimate Performance Requirements | 13 | CB | 36 | | | | 36 | | | | |
| | | BA | 24 | | | | 24 | | | | |
| | | CT | 100 | | | | 100 | | | | |
| Update the Data Model | 5 | BA | 40 | | | | 40 | | | | |
| | | CB | 16 | | | | 16 | | | | |
| | | CT | 40 | | | | 40 | | | | |
| **Produce User Reqmnts. Document** | | | | | | | | | | | |
| Gather System Specifications | 17 | BA | 120 | 120 | | | | | | | |
| | | CB | 24 | 24 | | | | | | | |
| | | CT | 132 | 132 | | | | | | | |
| Distribute the Draft Specifications | 2 | BA | 16 | 16 | | | | | | | |
| | | CT | 16 | 16 | | | | | | | |
| **Assess Implementation Reqmnts.** | | | | | | | | | | | |
| Assess Technical Issues | 6 | PM | 16 | | | | 5 | 11 | | | |
| | | BA | 16 | | | | 6 | 10 | | | |
| | | CB | 16 | | | | 6 | 10 | | | |
| | | CT | 48 | | | | 16 | 32 | | | |
| Determine Design Approach | 3 | PM | 8 | | | | | 8 | | | |
| | | BA | 16 | | | | | 16 | | | |
| | | CB | 16 | | | | | 16 | | | |
| | | CT | 24 | | | | | 24 | | | |

| B.E.P.S. Task Name | Task Dura. | Res. Abb. | Total Est. | Jul | Aug | Sep | Oct | Nov | Dec | Jan | Feb |
|---|---|---|---|---|---|---|---|---|---|---|---|
| **Business System Analysis** | | | | | | | | | | | |
| **User Review of Requirements** | | | | | | | | | | | |
| Prepare for User Reviews | 4 | BA | 32 | | | | | 32 | | | |
| | | PM | 16 | | | | | 16 | | | |
| | | CB | 32 | | | | | 32 | | | |
| | | CT | 16 | | | | | 16 | | | |
| Conduct User Reviews | 4 | BA | 32 | | | | | 32 | | | |
| | | CM | 16 | | | | | 16 | | | |
| | | CB | 32 | | | | | 32 | | | |
| | | CU | 32 | | | | | 32 | | | |
| **Decide Changes & Impl. Strategy** | | | | | | | | | | | |
| Accept User Changes | 4 | PM | 32 | 32 | | | | | | | |
| | | BA | 32 | 32 | | | | | | | |
| | | CM | 32 | 32 | | | | | | | |
| | | CB | 32 | 32 | | | | | | | |
| Document Sponsor Decisions | 2 | BA | 16 | 16 | | | | | | | |
| | | CB | 16 | 16 | | | | | | | |
| **Plan Technical Design Phase** | | | | | | | | | | | |
| Develop the Technical Design Plan | 18 | PM | 60 | 60 | | | | | | | |
| | | BA | 80 | 80 | | | | | | | |
| BSA Complete | | | | | | | | | | | |
| **Techncial Design** | | | | | | | | | | | |
| SUMMARY Technical Design | 29 | TEAM | 1,800 | | | | | | | | |
| **Construction** | | | | | | | | | | | |
| SUMMARY Construction | 55 | TEAM | 3,000 | | | | | | | | |
| **User Testing** | | | | | | | | | | | |
| SUMMARY User Testing | 34 | TEAM | 1,800 | | | | | | | | |
| **Transition** | | | | | | | | | | | |
| SUMMARY Transition | 30 | TEAM | 1,200 | | | | | | | | |
| Totals | | | 10,774 | 1,523 | 504 | 303 | 310 | 335 | | | |
| | | | | | | | | | | | |
| Project Manager | PM | 8.0 | 464 | 223 | 108 | 93 | 5 | 35 | | | |
| Business Analyst | BA | 8.0 | 994 | 582 | 132 | 104 | 86 | 90 | | | |
| Customer Business Expert | CB | 8.0 | 614 | 372 | 82 | 12 | 58 | 90 | | | |
| Consultants - Technical | CT | 8.0 | 822 | 314 | 182 | 94 | 161 | 72 | | | |
| Customer Manager | CM | 8.0 | 48 | 32 | 0 | 0 | 0 | 16 | | | |
| Customer Users | CU | 8.0 | 32 | | | | | 32 | | | |
| TEAM | TEAM | 8.0 | 7,800 | | | | | | | | |
| Totals | | | 10,774 | 1,523 | 504 | 303 | 310 | 335 | | | |

Thorough project plans make tracking and managing the project easier and more efficient, facilitates the orientation of new team members (including a new project manager), and will greatly benefit post-project evaluation.

## The 80-Hour Rule and Systems Development Life Cycles

The systems development life cycles that you have in place within your organization should serve as a guide to planning a project. This SDLC helps to create the work breakdown structure. A project manager can review the project against the appropriate phase and examine the recommended activities and tasks as a checklist for the project. This checklist will then lead the project manager directly into breaking the project down with the 80-Hour Rule.

## Dependencies and Critical Paths

When one task of a project depends upon the completion of another, that task relationship is one of the project's *dependencies*. About 95% of these dependencies in information technology are what we call *finish-start relationships*, meaning that one task cannot be started until the other is finished. There is a finish-start relationship between programming specs and actual programming. You cannot (or should not) start coding a program until you have defined the specifications for that program. Many of us have found it best to completely finish taking off our clothes before we start taking a shower or bath: a finish-start relationship from our worldly lives.

The project manager is responsible for identifying such dependencies within a project. The relationship of every task to others in the project should be noted. Every task should have a task preceding it and a task following it. Once this has been accomplished, one of the automated scheduling routines in your software package can create the network diagrams that will show the *critical path(s)*. The critical path is that series of sequential, dependent tasks that must begin and end on the planned dates in order for the project to be completed by the earliest possible delivery date.

Today's technology provides us with inexpensive, readily accessible tools to make our lives easier and more effective. The most basic project management software provides the ability to declare task dependencies and calculate critical paths. It is increasingly difficult or impossible to plan, schedule, and manage a relatively complex project to a successful conclusion without using an automated process.

The principal reasons for identifying dependencies and critical paths are the following:

1. It makes little difference whether you have resource availability if a task cannot be worked on because it is awaiting the completion of another. Clearly there are certain tasks that must precede others. You cannot accurately schedule a project unless you have identified dependencies.

2. In order to keep a project on schedule and on budget, the project manager must remain focused on the tasks in the critical path(s), because if one of these task slips, the project slips.

3. When change occurs, as it most surely will, you can accurately assess its impact only if you have mapped out the dependencies and critical paths.

In the world of information technology, critical paths and dependencies are usually best shown through networking diagrams generated through what are called Precedence Diagramming Methods. The details of this procedural technique are outside the scope of this book. Successful project managers will familiarize themselves with these processes to increase their abilities to manage dependencies and critical paths.

## Scheduling Resources

When you are breaking the job down into tasks of 80 hours or less, it is finally time to schedule some of those people you involved in Chapter 2.

If you are working with scheduling or project management software, the staff resources you have identified are logged into the software and it will schedule people to tasks. You will, of course, need to make some adjustments. No automated process we have worked with has ever given us a perfect schedule without some "tweaking." Even if you do not actually have people for the project yet, you want to prepare a schedule demonstrating a desired number of people on the project team.

When scheduling resources, one problem with automated procedures becomes evident. You give the computer a name, and it blindly plugs it into all the appropriate slots. It does not think about the individual and the assignment. It does not ask, "Does this task offer a good learning experience? Is the timing right considering what the person has just gone through on a previous assignment? Will he or she get along with the others on the team?" Don't forget that you are dealing with people when you make schedule assignments. The computer is a great aid, but it has no discriminating faculties. As project manager, it is your responsibility to supply the intelligence and humanity to the management of a project.

If you are not using scheduling software, you assign each individual appropriate tasks until all tasks and resource time are accounted for. This manual process can become quite laborious on a large or complex project. Many of us did it for years using the stubby pencil and eraser approach, and many of us are not anxious to return to those days.

*Adding more people to a late project usually makes it later.*

## Square Root Rule

One could get quite wrapped up in trying to determine the maximum number of people to put on a project. Added resources mean added communication links that grow like spider webs in geometric profusion. Resource scheduling is an exercise in logic that depends upon the nature of the project, the availability of people, the staff's skill levels in the development techniques, their familiarity with the business applications, project schedule demands, and a host of other personal and organizational interests.

There is a rule of thumb used to help identify the maximum number of people that a project can withstand: the maximum number of people on a project should not exceed the square root of the number of elapsed person-months to complete the project. (This calculation *excludes* project management time.) To apply the rule

1. Determine the total effort-hours of all the tasks, 1,200 hours for example.

2. Multiply effort-hours from the above example by the productivity factor (1.25) to get elapsed hours.

1,200 x 1.25 = 1,500 elapsed hours

3. Divide the elapsed hours by 168 (elapsed hours in a month) to get elapsed person-months.

1,500 / 168 = 8.93

4. Take the square root of the person-months to determine the maximum number of people on the project.

$\sqrt{8.93} = 2.98$

5. Round this number up to whole people instead of looking for someone who is a few hundredths off.

Three people would be the most you would want to have on this example project at any one time. Again, this is a rule of thumb, and every rule has its exceptions.

## Team Self-Management in Implementing the 80-Hour Rule

During the course of developing the Principles of Productivity Management, we tried many different techniques for implementing the 80-Hour Rule and settled on what follows as the most effective approach.

It is not the project manager's job to break the project down into 80-hour deliverable tasks; it is the job of the team members. Your job as project manager is to assign a meaningful and significant body of work to a team member and to request that he or she break it down using the 80-Hour Rule. Treat that portion of the job as if you were subcontracting it out.

Team members implementing the 80-Hour Rule will need to use the same approach for their tasks as the project manager uses for the whole project. The individual should prepare (1) a plan that produces a tangible deliverable product every 80 hours or less, (2) an estimate in effort-hours of all the tasks to be performed, and (3) a schedule reflecting start and complete dates for each task. They may have to break some large programs into modules, or some large analysis or design tasks into smaller business functions.

If the *team* breaks the job down, the plan will be *theirs,* not yours, and will more likely be correct. And because it is "their plan," they will have a higher level of commitment to implementing it. In the discussion of Maslow's Hierarchy of Needs, we identified self-actualization as the highest-level motivator. This approach to the 80-Hour Rule is a means to enable self-actualization.

Since team members identify many separate tasks when applying the 80-Hour Rule, they have many opportunities to succeed. A programmer with 20 clearly defined tasks has 20 opportunities to achieve success. Twenty tasks of 80 hours' duration or less are much better than one task of 1,600 hours. Each programmer is, in effect, managing him- or herself. Even if some activities fall behind schedule, he or she can manage others so that the whole assignment is completed on or close to budget and schedule. And the project manager has a more realistic and accurate appraisal of project status and is better positioned to make any necessary adjustments.

Members of a project team should be masters of their domains to the extent that is possible and to the extent that they desire. For those who thrive on practicing self-management, the project manager must provide every opportunity to do so. What this means is that if an individual wants to have more control, he or she should be responsible for implementing the 80-Hour Rule for his or her tasks.

Some managers are against permitting this level of self-management, suspecting that people will pad their estimates unreasonably so they can coast through a project. The reality is quite the opposite. Most people, in fact, are more likely to *underestimate* the time it will take them to do a task.

The 80-Hour Rule provides multiple opportunities for recognition and reward for team members. People want to do a good job and they want to know they are doing a good job.

When they have a deliverable product due every two weeks, they get the reward of having satisfactorily completed something every two weeks. Knowing that a task is done and seeing the tangible progress by moving on to the next one is rewarding to the team and keeps the project moving along briskly and with high morale.

## Maintaining a 90-Day Rolling Forecast

One cannot expect that a large project could be completely broken down into tasks of 80 hours or less from the very beginning. It would be unreasonable to expect any level of accuracy for activities that will not be taking place for a year— or even six months. Eighty-hour job breakdown is not done until real people are actually assigned to the job. This level of detail is usually available only for about 90 days into the immediate future (the same 90-day window used for precise estimates discussed in Chapter 3).

At Keane, we maintain such a *90-day rolling forecast* on all projects. We begin a project with three months' worth of detailed, 80-hour task plans and then, at the end of the first month, we have the team members do another month's worth of detailed planning. This will happen at the end of each month so we always have 90 days' worth of detailed tasks ready to assign.

## Benefits of the 80-Hour Rule

Projects don't suddenly become behind schedule and over budget. Have you ever left a perfectly good project one evening and come in the next morning to find it was eight weeks late and thousands of dollars over budget? Probably not. They drift off course in bits and pieces. If you measure tasks every 80 hours or less, however, the longest you go before knowing that there is some kind of problem is two weeks. And with two weeks' notice, you can usually correct a problem. Waiting much longer tends to amplify the problem geometrically.

One more advantage to the 80-Hour Rule is that it allows you to identify any potential problems with new people very quickly. Before using the 80-Hour Rule, we often brought someone new onto a project and gave them tasks that would take a month or even several months to complete only to discover that the individual was not as strong in a technical area as we anticipated or were led to believe. Or perhaps we failed to give them a good understanding of the application and of what was expected. If the project is governed by the 80-Hour Rule, we know if there are any problems and can address them after a maximum of two weeks.

## Planning under Special Circumstances

### Working with Mandated Completion Dates

While you might treasure being able to plan your project and freely decide the completion dates, the realities of life frequently introduce a mandated complete date by the customer. While many are genuine, some mandated dates are unnecessarily and unreasonably set by people more interested in their own self-aggrandizement than allotting the adequate amount of time to complete a project. Nevertheless, mandated dates are here to stay. On the bright side, with a mandated date, at least you have one less item to figure out. You know when the project is going to end.

Beware, however, the pitfalls that can accompany fixed completion dates. First, you must not allow the need for a specific, possibly unreasonable, completion date to cloud your estimates. It does not take less time to do a task because someone says, "Hurry up." The effort-hours you and the extended team estimated are the best guesses at how long the project's tasks will take. The effort-hours will not change unless functionality changes. If you want fewer effort-hours, you must reduce functionality; that is, you must eliminate tasks.

If you cannot reduce functionality and the date is fixed, you have only two alternatives: (1) increase the number of people, and/or (2) increase their hours on the job. Bringing in more people is an occasional solution to scheduling problems caused by mandated dates; however, throwing more bodies at a job does not always make it go faster. Each additional team member must be integrated into the project from technical, organizational, and interpersonal perspectives. There is a point when the addition of one more individual will so impact the communication complexities that it will have a detrimental effect on the project. This would be a good time to use the "square root rule" to determine the maximum number of people to involve on a job.

If adding more people is not an option, you must schedule those you already have in an overtime situation. It is dangerous, however, to *schedule* a project with overtime from the outset. Should any problems arise, you will have no leeway to adjust for them. If you absolutely must schedule with overtime, be sure that everyone is aware of what and how

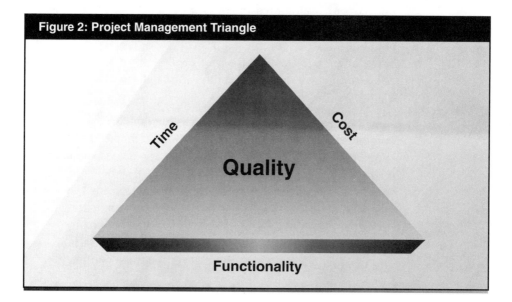

**Figure 2: Project Management Triangle**

much is expected from them up front. People deal with overtime much better if they know what it is from the beginning; then they can plan their lives around it with some semblance of order. Be sure also to tell them the expected duration of the overtime. If it is going to be eight extra hours a week for the next 20 weeks, tell them well in advance. Don't just keep dragging it out from week to week with "Just one more week, folks."

Again, the basic triangle (figure 2) demonstrates the interdependent variables that you can adjust when managing a project: functionality, time, and cost (in effort-hours or dollars).

## Fast-Tracking, Crashing, and Overtime

Sometimes a project must be completed sooner than its previously accepted estimated date of completion. There are some basic approaches you can use to accommodate such a need. Again, do not automatically assume that you can speed up the schedule by simply assigning more people to the project. Putting more people on a late project will usually make it later.

Since time is now not an option, recalling the project management triangle, only cost (or resources) and functionality can be considered. At Keane, we have arrived at a sequence in which to consider measures for expediting a project. That sequence appears below.

1. Review dependencies of those tasks on the critical path(s) to see where dependencies might be eliminated or overlap may be possible. This process is commonly referred to as *fast-tracking* and is best handled through project management software. *Overlap* implies that even though there is a finish-start relationship between tasks, some amount of simultaneous work is permissible. Detailed coverage of Critical Path Methodology and the concepts of overlap and lag is widely available in commercial literature.

2. Determine which tasks might benefit from ***crashing.*** Crashing is decreasing the elapsed time of a task by assigning more resources to it. Consider these tasks from the perspectives of *time gain* and *cost.* Which tasks will afford the largest time gain if we assign more resources and what are the increased costs associated with this effort? Choose the most effective combination.

3. Explore the benefit of augmenting the existing resources through ***overtime.*** Begin by adding about five hours of availability per week to those individuals who have tasks on the critical path. This could eventually be increased to 12 or 15 hours depending on what the team members will accept. Obviously, there is room to add considerably more hours than that but the results begin to negate themselves beyond this point through more errors and overextension of the team.

4. If the required date still has not been met after adopting the above measures, consider reducing functionality. What tasks can be eliminated from the project and possibly moved to another later project? Warning: do not attempt to eliminate or reduce *testing;* this will only increase the time it will take to actually complete the project. A better approach is to work closely with the customer and agree on what functions could be eliminated or postponed.

Using the above sequence allows you to consider each technique individually and gain full advantage from it before exploring the next. Any combination of the above approaches may help you adjust to a shifting completion date.

# Managing Progress

## Maintaining Control of a Project

Consider this scenario: a new project manager was asked to stop by our regional office in order to do a brief review on the status of his project. He said he would "run the numbers" and make sure everything was up-to-date before coming in. This was a medium-sized project of six people over five months and had about a $250,000 estimate to complete. He came in somewhat late the next morning disheveled and anxious. Before we could even say, "Good morning," he announced that he was unprepared to do the review; he was terribly sorry but he was off by 30 dollars, and he would keep trying. He said he would be back the next day or maybe later that night.

The problem here is that this project manager had become too focused on the project accounting and the use of the project management software. A $30 discrepancy on a quarter-million dollar project is not too bad. We would have gladly given him the 30 dollars. (Or, of course, taken it from him if he was over.) The lesson is *keep your focus on the deliverable products*. Don't become a bean counter. We sometimes find that project managers get so wrapped up in the accounting, reconciliation, and reporting that they forget they are supposed to be managing people and a project.

This project manager had also slipped into a fundamental misunderstanding about his project's objectives. The success of this project was not specifically tied to on-time, on-budget completion. The most important critical success factor to the customer was that the development team work closely with the users to identify requirements for the virtual-office communication functions that would enable the department to double in size over the following two years. Managing to the budget was of relatively low priority.

In another instance, a project manager complained that her project was drifting, and although she was working as hard as she could and was putting in long hours, she seemed unable to stop it from getting later and later. When we visited her the next day, we found her up to her elbows helping the analysts with design specs and coding one of the major update programs.

She had succumbed to another one of the basic traps of project management: under stress, we regress. As project pressures mounted, she regressed to doing the technical activities that got her promoted to the project management position—programming and writing specs. She was so close to the trees that she could no longer see the forest around her. She was neglecting to maintain a management perspective of the entire project as she became deeply involved helping out in technical areas. Certainly there may be times when the right thing to do is roll up your sleeves and help with technical tasks, but not to the detriment of management. Project managers must manage first and contribute second—even if they are the sole member of a one-person project team.

## Project Status Reporting

Monitoring progress with the 80-Hour Rule in place is relatively simple, since every week or two the team should be delivering completed products. Outside of the natural review process of evaluating the deliverables, however, you should establish a firm weekly reporting schedule. Weekly progress reports (exhibit 10), whether a deliverable is completed or not, are the most effective way for a project manager to remain closely connected to and aware of the project's progress—and potential problems.

Everyone on the extended project team should be aware that the reporting schedule for the project is weekly with no exceptions. Getting those weekly project status reports will test all your skills, experience, saintliness, patience, threats, and evil, conniving ways. Let the schedule be known at the very beginning of the project, enforce it throughout, and insist that it be a mandate for *everyone* involved with the project.

Many project managers like to have the project team's weekly status reports by 3:00 p.m. on Friday when the information is still fresh in the team members' minds. This gives the project manager the opportunity to think about project status over the weekend. This is not necessarily to encourage weekend work

## Exhibit 9: Weekly Timesheet

| Task ID | Tasks for Business Analyst Task Name | Period Start: 12/25/95<br>Period End: 12/31/95<br>Start | End | Estimate for Current Period | Actual Hours to Date | Actual Hours This Week | Est. to Comp. |
|---|---|---|---|---|---|---|---|
| **W030** | **Business System Analysis** | | | | | | |
| W030 | **Prepare Diagrams** | | | | | | |
| W030 | Develop the Data Model | 7/3 | 7/21 | 120 | | 0 | 120 |
| W030 | Develop the Process Model | 7/24 | 8/23 | 180 | | 0 | 180 |
| W030 | **Generate Functional/Data Reqmnts.** | | | | | | |
| W030 | Write the Primitive Process Specifications | 7/3 | 7/27 | 150 | | 0 | 150 |
| W030 | Reconcile the Process and Data Models | 9/13 | 10/3 | 120 | | 0 | 120 |
| W030 | **Generate Performance Reqmnts.** | | | | | | |
| W030 | Estimate Performance Requirements | 10/4 | 10/20 | 24 | | 0 | 24 |
| W030 | Update the Data Model | 10/23 | 10/27 | 40 | | 0 | 40 |
| W030 | **Produce User Reqmnts. Document** | | | | | | |
| W030 | Gather System Specifications | 7/3 | 7/25 | 120 | | 0 | 120 |
| W030 | Distribute the Draft Specifications | 7/26 | 7/27 | 16 | | 0 | 16 |
| W030 | **Assess Implementation Reqmnts.** | | | | | | |
| W030 | Assess Technical Issues | 10/30 | 11/6 | 16 | | 0 | 16 |
| W030 | Determine Design Approach | 11/7 | 11/9 | 16 | | 0 | 16 |
| W030 | **User Review of Requirements** | | | | | | |
| W030 | Prepare for User Reviews | 11/10 | 11/15 | 32 | | 0 | 32 |
| W030 | Conduct User Reviews | 11/16 | 11/21 | 32 | | 0 | 32 |
| W030 | **Decide Changes & Impl. Strategy** | | | | | | |
| W030 | Accept User Changes | 7/3 | 7/6 | 32 | | 0 | 32 |
| W030 | Document Sponsor Decisions | 7/7 | 7/10 | 16 | | 0 | 16 |
| W030 | **Plan Technical Design Phase** | | | | | | |
| W030 | Develop the Technical Design Plan | 7/3 | 7/26 | 80 | | 0 | 80 |
| Totals | | | | 994 | 0 | | 994 |

but to ensure that there is adequate time for thought, which can then lead to effective action. A project manager's greatest worth is in analyzing activity and taking the necessary actions to maintain meaningful progress. The best thinking takes a little time (like a weekend), and the decisions that you implement on Monday morning are likely to be the better for it.

You should avoid status reporting at the beginning of the week. Monday mornings tend to be chaotic. Collecting status reports, reviewing them in detail, and making intelligent decisions under conditions of chaos is difficult to impossible. Generally speaking, any weekly schedule is okay as long as it provides ample time for reflection and logical decision making.

The purpose of weekly status reporting is to

1. Help all members become accomplished in self-management;

2. Communicate the previous week's and total accomplishments to plan;

3. Identify problems and opportunities;

4. Provide for scheduling adjustments;

5. Identify changes; and

6. Document activity for future planning.

No matter what software or manual methods are used, the focus of the status reports should be on the following items:

1. What products were completed? What products were started?

2. What is the revised estimated time to complete tasks?

   (Team members should take the time to reestimate their tasks weekly so you have an accurate picture of the whole project. You should discourage the tendency to simply let project management software subtract time spent to date from the original estimate.

# Weekly Progress Report

**KEANE**

To: _____  Week Ending: _____

From: _____  Client Name: _____

Project Name: _____  Client No.: _____ Proj. No.: _____

The products I delivered this week are:

The products I planned to deliver this week were:

My plan to deliver next week is:

This week I lost time due to: (specify hours)

Problems that may cause me future lost time are:

Hours billed this week are:

| Task | Est. Hours | Hrs. This Week | Hrs. to Date | Hrs. to Complete | On Calendar Schedule |
|------|-----------|----------------|--------------|------------------|----------------------|
|      |           |                |              |                  |                      |
|      |           |                |              |                  |                      |
|      |           |                |              |                  |                      |
|      |           |                |              |                  |                      |

3. What existing or potential problems is the team aware of?

4. What non-compliance changes are affecting the team on the project?

The exact nature of the weekly status reports will be largely determined by the project management software and the policies and procedures of the organization. The reporting schedules, formats, and report recipients for a project should be identified in the statement of work. After collecting, analyzing, and evaluating the status information, the project manager's job is to make decisions or suggestions regarding changes to be made—if changes are necessary—to keep the project on track. To keep the project under control, you must see regular evidence of progress as reported weekly through some form of status reporting. Above all, the purpose of this reporting activity is to allow the project manager to manage the project to a successful conclusion.

The reporting mechanism should alert you if someone is likely to miss a deliverable. A perceptive, inquiring project manager will be able to analyze information, determine corrective actions, and provide the leadership to effect the necessary change. If a team member does miss a deliverable, first find out the *real* reason that it occurred, then seek to resolve the problem.

Your greatest worth as a project manager is in understanding what is going on and taking the necessary actions to maintain meaningful progress. Progress reporting is certainly a beneficial and required step of the project management process, but it does not fully constitute management. Project managers can probably anticipate that they will spend four to eight hours per week for the above progress reporting tasks. Concern yourself more with specific deliverable products than simply with hours or dollars expended. And don't forget that you are dealing with people who need occasional attention. Even criticism is better than nothing. People need to know how they are doing.

## The Follow-Up File and Project Control Book

You can maximize project control by giving out the right-sized tasks and ensure that they get done. The ability to distribute tasks of the correct size and subsequently to check that they are completed is an important leadership skill with the 80-Hour Rule. Maintaining some form of follow-up file can be a great help to a project manager. Few of us are capable of remembering all of the many tasks that we have to do. Failure to follow up thoroughly and in a timely fashion will probably be one of the biggest problems you will face as a manager. Begin developing good follow-up and control techniques very early in your project management career.

Another important element of successful project control and status reporting is the upkeep of the Project Control Book, which contains management-oriented material, usually maintained in a three-ring binder. Each project should have its own Project Control Book.

The Project Control Book must be maintained on a weekly basis in conjunction with progress reporting. Below is a checklist for the contents of the Project Control Book.

1. At project initiation:

    a. Statement of Work

    b. Original plan

    c. Deliverables schedules

2. Added weekly:

    a. The updated plan

    b. Posted deliverables schedules

    c. Updated team member and summary status reports

    d. Management status reports

    e. Team status reports

    f. Timesheets, expenses, etc.

3. Added as needed:

   a. Submitted task completion notices

   b. Approved task completion notices

   c. Submitted change requests

   d. Approved change requests

   e. Miscellaneous correspondence, meeting minutes, etc.

## Trend Analysis

*Trend analysis* refers to the process of tracking progress in order to forecast its impact on the project. Weekly reporting in quantitative (time/dollars spent) and narrative form is the most accurate and effective method of monitoring progress on a project. But there are other techniques that can augment the weekly reports and the most common are listed below:

- Earned Value Analysis (explained below)

- High-risk task forecasts

- Trend analysis versus next period reporting

- Estimate-to-complete summaries

- Critically late task analysis

*Earned Value Analysis* is one widely used trend analysis technique in which you track progress by measuring the value a project accrues as tasks are performed on it. As each deliverable is created, the dollar value of the project increases. This technique enables you to construct a quantitative model of the project with which you forecast a final outcome and compare to the Performance Measurement Baseline set during the estimating stage. Earned Value Analysis allows you to track not only costs for resource hours, but also any direct expenses for materials, equipment, travel, etc., that will have an effect on the final budget.

There are many techniques besides earned value that may be employed to track progress and predict trends. Even simple bar charts to illustrate resources expended can be very effective in helping to spot problems before they become serious. As project manager, you should find which techniques work best for you and use them consistently.

## Quality Assurance

*Software Quality Assurance* is also a major issue within most software development organizations. None of us want our customers adversely effected by poor quality software.

As you might expect, in an organization the size of Keane (currently 4,500 Information Systems managers and technicians), we encounter widely varying forms of quality assurance. Finding an appropriate quality assurance process is no problem; there are plenty out there. The problem is in the lack of doing. The project manager must build quality assurance procedures into the project from the very beginning. Those procedures must be followed throughout the project life. When each deliverable has its own set of quality checks, consistent application of quality assurance procedures is guaranteed.

There is no discounting the fact that quality assurance costs time and money. Whether it pays for itself through increased profits and fewer defects is difficult to prove objectively, but our subjective observations are (1) adherence to software quality assurance procedures is a significant contributor to many organizations' continued success and profitability, and (2) there is frequently a lack of quality assurance procedures in those organizations struggling with projects, profitability, and continued organizational existence.

## Automated Tools in Tracking the Project

Today's projects demand a higher level of complexity and a shorter term to completion than ever before. The expectation is that you can do more, faster, with less. This being the case, automated tools are almost indispensable. The 80-Hour Rule does not change as we do more, faster. People will continue to perform best when they focus on smaller activities, gaining approval for successfully completed tasks.

Automated tools currently make their most significant contribution in the project planning process, but they are also of great value in tracking the project and managing change. They simplify

- Determining your organization's or department's rate of productivity by month and year

- Recording progress on the project

- Measuring progress and indicating variances

- Forecasting trends and estimates to complete

- Making changes to existing plans

- Providing the historical records for subsequent evaluation and improvement.

Virtually all project management software readily supports the basic components of Productivity Management. There are some problems associated with using software for project tracking and reporting, and they often stem from the fact that computers cannot process nondata information. The essential nature of the problems are manifest in two areas:

1. A computer cannot consider individual and personal issues. (Suzanne has been scheduled to work overtime on the same night that she has a final exam for a statistics class.)

2. A computer does not necessarily practice good management. (In order to use a project as an opportunity for training in a new GUI language, you have decided to put two people on one program. The automated management package would assign one person to the task.)

These issues can be successfully addressed, but the project manager must first consider them rather than just letting the software blindly assign resources and schedule tasks. Project management software will prepare plans and estimates, regularly post effort-hours against these plans, create status reports, and prepare management summaries with little or no human intervention, but too much reliance on the software output may cause you to forget individual and managerial issues. First, make the management decisions, then devise a way for the software to do it.

## Chapter Summary: Break the Job Down Using the 80-Hour Rule

1. All projects can be broken down into individual tasks, none of which should require more than 80 elapsed hours for a deliverable product to be produced.

2. Breaking the job down should result in deliverable products that are visible and tangible.

3. Each organization must determine what its productivity level is by capturing and measuring time actually spent on projects over the course of a year.

4. Effort-hours refers to the unpadded hours estimated or actually spent in completing a task.

   Elapsed time refers to the calendar time it takes to complete those effort-hours.

5. Project plans and progress should be reflected on Gantt charts and Weekly Progress Reports.

   Team members should be able to report progress narratively and quantitatively.

6. Project tasks possess dependent relationships, usually falling into the category of finish-start relationships. Identifying these relationships allows you to define the critical path(s).

7.  Project management should focus on the critical path(s).

8.  The "square root rule" can be used as a guide to help determine the maximum number of people that should be on a project.

9.  Every team member should set his or her own plans and be responsible for tracking his or her own progress against those plans.

10. Breaking activities down into tasks of 80 hours or less provides multiple opportunities for recognition and reward.

11. Maintain a 90-day rolling forecast of the project broken down into deliverables 80 hours or less.

12. Fast-tracking, overtime, and crashing are techniques that can help a project that is behind schedule.

13. Project managers must focus on product deliverables and not just the measurement of hours and dollars.

14. It is the project manager's responsibility to see that progress is accurately reported on a weekly basis.

15. The project manager is responsible for initiating and maintaining the Project Control Book.

16. There are many forms of automated trend analysis available (such as Earned Value Analysis) that can help predict probable project, phase, activity, or task outcome.

17. Automated project management software does not employ personnel management skills. The project manager must supply those skills.

# 5 Principle Five: Establish a Change Procedure

# Establish a Change Procedure

It's no wonder that many software developers find it difficult to welcome changes to a project. Changes can wreak havoc on a project if they are improperly managed: they have been known to balloon budgets and schedules; destroy the design integrity of systems; and breed animosity among customers, the development team, and all associated management. But it is foolish to pretend that you could work on a project without encountering changes in any number of areas—customer need, schedule, budget. Fortunately, there is a beneficial and painless way to accommodate changes to a project. Project managers who have defined the job in detail and who establish a *change procedure* will be able to evaluate changes as soon as they occur. When change is recognized and managed, it can create opportunities rather than problems. It can improve the system rather than undermine it.

There are two types of changes that occur on a project: *design changes* and *non-compliance changes,* and each type must be managed differently. Simply stated, design changes are welcome and non-compliance changes are not.

## Handling Design Changes

### What is a Design Change?

*Design changes* are improvements or corrections to the system design after the initial specifications have been approved. Such changes are a natural outcome of the design process and should be encouraged.

Managers frequently fail to regard design changes as a normal part of the systems development process but view them, rather, as direct causes of overruns and loss of control. Although freezing specifications and prohibiting changes to a project may *seem* like the way to maintain control, it is seldom a reasonable or acceptable approach. A healthier and more realistic attitude is to view system design as a fluid process of which change is an inherent part. The increasing complexity of software development coupled with the varying interests of multiple customers make it virtually impossible to foresee all details of development at the beginning. Change is inevitable.

Design change tends to fall into specific categories, and recognizing the more common groupings can be of benefit in helping to estimate the time and cost impact of change, determine its cost benefit, and manage it to a successful implementation. Some of the more common reasons for design changes are listed below with an example to illustrate each one.

- New or varying business opportunities arise.

  A women's blouse manufacturer introduced a new product line at the same time as a new payables and receivables package was being installed. The new product line required invoicing and record keeping that was different from that of the new package.

- Someone comes up with a better way of doing something.

  After viewing sample output from new screen layouts, the customer realized that two of the screens could be combined to make data entry much more efficient.

- There are errors in understanding or communication.

  The wrong database was chosen as input to the system, and several large programs required extensive changes.

- The originally selected approach has proven unwieldy or impossible.

  A manufacturer intended for the code on their product to identify both the product and the manufacturing plant location. The single code was not possible because the product code was limited to six digits, but there were more than 1,700,000 potential combinations. A second code was required to identify place of manufacture.

- Local, state, or federal regulations have created new requirements.

  New SEC regulations restricted a bank from issuing certain types of savings certificates in three contiguous states where they were planning on doing business.

- Organizational changes have introduced new players with different views.

  A new vice president decided not to share the new sales reporting system being developed for his business unit. All recognition of sales from two other business units had to be removed from the system, which was already in final acceptance testing.

- Better software or hardware technology has become available.

  A customer decided that one of two hardware platforms would be eliminated because better development software was available from the vendor. The decision affected three systems in various stages of development on the platform to be eliminated.

## Baselining

The key to measuring change on a project—that is, knowing when change is occurring—is the Performance Measurement Baseline. As discussed in Chapter 3, "Estimate the Time and Costs," the baseline is the original estimate of dollars and hours against which you track progress. Without the baseline to measure against, you would always be on schedule—or always off schedule; no one would know because there would really be no schedule.

The two most common problems that project managers seem to have with a Performance Measurement Baseline are that (1) they simply don't create one, and (2) if they do create one, they refuse to change it. The first problem is often a result of the notion that *planning* is equivalent to *commitment*. Wary project managers worry that if they develop a baselined project plan and put it in writing, they will be expected to adhere exactly to that plan. This can be frightening because it introduces the possibility of failure. You should not, however, think of baselines in those terms. The baseline does not present an opportunity for failure but rather the best opportunity for the success of a project. The baseline is the instrument that lets the customers and your managers know that you are succeeding. Without it, the project cannot and will not be completed on time, within budget, or according to whatever criteria have been established.

The baseline *will* require revision. The *original* Performance Measurement Baseline will always be maintained as the progress measurement reference over the life of the project and for final project review. But since projects change, a new baseline must occasionally be drafted to reflect the revised estimate. Any baseline subsequent to the PMB is referred to as the *revised* or *current baseline*.

Knowing when to revise the baseline comes from experience. Sometimes it is after one significant change to the project. In other instances it may be as a result of an accumulation of many small changes over several months. You should not be overly protective of your original baseline. If changes require adjustment of the baseline, recognize them and revise. Some project managers develop a standard percentage of deviation from the PMB as an indicator for when to revise. If, for example, the total project variance is 10% to 20% from the existing baseline, they introduce a new baseline. Measuring against a baseline that bears no resemblance to reality has no use.

## Include a "Change Budget" in the Original Estimate

Since you know that change will occur, it makes sense to budget for it. At Keane, we include a *change budget* in the original estimate. The purpose of the change budget is to provide an appropriation (in dollars or hours) the project manager can draw from without having to gain approval from the governor of the purse strings. If refinancing is required for every minor change to the project, effective progress will be impeded.

Some people use other terms such as "contingency funds" and "management reserve" in referring to funds to accommodate change; these terms are not as explicit as "change budget" and are therefore less desirable. "Contingency" tends to connote an appropriation for a risk-oriented eventuality such as pending litigation or product liability. "Management reserve" could mean anything. "Change budget" says exactly what it means and alerts all parties of the realistic expectations for change.

Once the estimate of effort-hours and/or dollars for the entire project (which will then serve as the original Performance Measurement Baseline) is complete, a change budget is fixed as an additional percentage amount. The estimate plus the change budget is the total ***Budget at Completion.*** Figure 8 illustrates a budgeted project plan with a change budget of about 10%. The upper line represents the total estimated cost to complete the project and the lower line represents the Performance Measurement Baseline. The space between the two lines represents the change budget.

If changes are not tracked against a separate budget, you never know whether the original estimate was in error because of poor estimating or because of the magnitude of change that occurred. To improve skills in estimating and in managing change, the two must be tracked separately. If, for example, you find that your estimates were off because of excessive change, it may be an indication that you are not spending enough time in the analysis or design phases ... or that you did not have the right people involved identifying requirements. If changes are being managed against a fixed change budget, the decreasingly available amount will always be measurable and obvious.

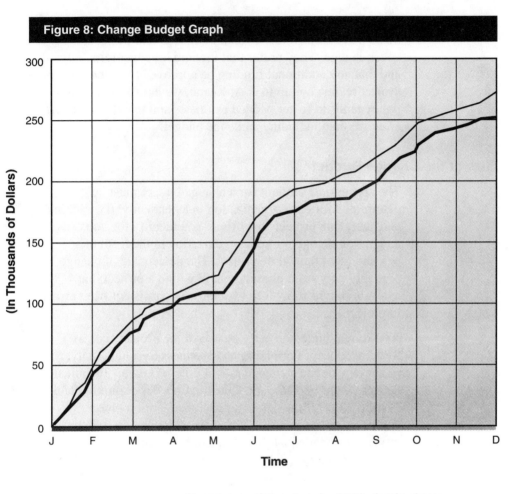

**Figure 8: Change Budget Graph**

——— Budget at completion - includes 10% budget for change

**▬▬▬** Estimate to complete (Project/Performance Measurement Baseline)

Some organizations will find it difficult to accept the concept that a percentage of the overall budget should be set aside to cover change. They prefer that the initial budget remain fixed and that any additional funding be approved by some form of project review committee. At Keane, we have found that this policy tends to foster padded estimates and that it is less cost-effective than including a change budget.

## Size of the Change Budget

The appropriate amount for a change budget must be determined for each organization independently. By tracking and analyzing projects over time, you identify the consistent amount of change for your organization in the form of a percentage of the whole project. The percentage of change will probably vary from phase to phase within a project, but analysis should show it to be relatively consistent from project to project.

As a rough guide, the early phases of the project such as System Concept Formation and Business Systems Analysis might experience a change rate of 20% or higher. Technical Design might be 15%, and Construction (Programming and Testing) 10%. If the percentage of change for a phase approaches 35% or more, it may be an indication that the project was inadequately defined or that requirements were not well determined.

## Who Should Control the Change Budget?

In Chapter 2, we discussed the importance of customer involvement and the customer's role in managing the project. Here again, it is best if the customer controls the change budget. The customer is the best candidate to evaluate which changes deserve to be implemented. When they understand that changes require additional funds, they will be more likely to resist requesting trivial changes.

After almost five months on one project, we asked why none of a $32,000 change budget had been spent. The customer controlling the change budget responded, "I just wanted to save it in case something really important came up." The smaller the remaining budget, the harder everyone thinks before spending it.

Managing the change budget helps ensure active customer involvement in the project. Customers are often too willing to turn the project over to someone else, but it is not healthy for the customer to put the entire project in the hands of Information Systems. Most Information Systems people will gladly take over control of the project, the organization, the 48 contiguous states, and the federal government if you let them.

If the customer controls the change budget, they can evaluate requests for design changes keeping in mind the realistic costs that will result. Customers have the tendency to request the most changes toward the end of the project, because that is when more of the finished products are visible to the customer and desired improvements become more obvious. Generally, the later the change, the more expensive it is to implement. With this point emphasized, you should have no problem convincing the customer of the importance of thorough, up-front planning and of the customer's involvement in approving deliverables.

There also may be a third party who could control the change budget and provide an objective perspective—an accounting or auditing individual, for example. A balance of power can improve the entire process. As always, be sure to identify the individual controlling the change budget in writing at the beginning of the project, and note it in the statement of work.

## Negotiating Changes

Change is frequently a point of contention between the customer and the Information Systems organization, because they disagree on whether a particular function is a change or part of the initial agreement.

These conflicts can be mitigated to some extent through the preparation of detailed plans that are mutually developed, reviewed, and approved by everyone involved. If the job has been mutually defined, people have been rightly involved, the extended team has shared in the estimating process, and the project has been broken down into manageable pieces, then managing change will be much less a burden.

Negotiation skills are a necessary attribute for any successful project manager. Perhaps nowhere are they exercised more than in the activity of managing change. Much of this atmosphere of negotiation is caused by the unfortunate "we-they" relationship common between Information Systems and their customers. At the suggestion of change, the question of who is "at fault" surfaces almost immediately. Once the fault or source of change is determined, then the question of who pays is tackled. This attitude fosters animosity and divisiveness and is a severe impediment to effective project completion.

There are no easy answers at this point. Negotiations are based on mutual respect, previous relationships, individual skills, and a host of other professional, personal, and social attitudes. This is the key area in which the interrelationships of the Principles of Productivity Management come into play. Implementing them successfully will minimize debate and the practice of placing blame.

## Accommodating Requests for Change

A design change may be suggested by any involved party—customers, Information Systems personnel, or members of a technical or administrative support group. The project team evaluates the prospective change and estimates its effect on time, cost, and schedules. The approving authority then decides whether to accept the change.

To avoid misunderstandings, it is essential that all parties agree in advance on a formal procedure for handling change. This procedure should be identified in the statement of work. One such procedure is described below.

1. All parties agree in advance on the individual who will be responsible for final decisions regarding change.

2. A turnaround time for approvals is agreed upon.

3. The requester fills out a change request form (exhibit 11) stating the reason for the desired change and the benefits to be derived from it.

4. The change request form is submitted through a management control individual who passes it on to the project manager.

5. Designated project team members conduct a cost/benefit analysis. Since approval would mean that the change would be incorporated into the system, this analysis should be as detailed as the original estimate on which the entire project is based. At a minimum, the response should reflect an estimate for effort-hours, cost, resources required, and the change's effect on the project completion date. (Time and money devoted to analyzing a change request should come from the change budget. This is frequently a hotly negotiated item and must be agreed on in advance.)

6. The person(s) controlling the change budget approve or reject the change request. All approvals must be in writing. No change should be implemented until written approval is received. Remember: if it isn't in writing, it doesn't exist. Written approvals (and rejections) reduce the possibility of misunderstanding and ensure consistent documentation.

A formal procedure should be exercised at the earliest opportunity on even the most inconsequential changes. This sets an important precedent for the rest of the project and minimizes what can be an unending parade of small changes that nickel-and-dime the budget to an untimely demise.

# Change Request

**KEANE**

Client Name: _____Bristol_____  Client No.: _____

Project Name: _____BEPS_____  Project No.: _____

Requested By: _____Alex Kemper_____  Date: _____

Change No.: _____6 MKTG_____

**Description:**

Sales commission reports should indicate earnings to date as
a percentage of sales. This should appear on "on-line" system
and monthly summary reports.

This additional piece of information will help the managers evaluate
performance more effectively.

**Keane Acceptance:**

Approved By: _____  Title: _____  Date: _____

**Client Acceptance:**

Approved By: _____  Title: _____  Date: _____

# Handling Non-Compliance Changes

## What is a Non-compliance Change?

A *non-compliance change* is very different from a design change and is best defined as change resulting from a failure of someone to do what he or she previously committed to, or the failure of some previously planned event to occur. Someone or something is not complying with established arrangements.

A few examples of non-compliance changes are:

1. Milestones that are not met on schedule;

2. Failure of the customer to provide timely approval or rejection of products;

3. Vendor delays of products or services;

4. Project support services that are not available;

5. Previously promised test time that is not available;

6. Equipment that is out of service;

7. Software and systems that fail or are unavailable.

There are dozens of other non-compliance items, and each organization seems plagued with its own unique set of them. We have learned to formally log and track these non-compliance changes very closely.

The biggest difference between non-compliance changes and design changes is that non-compliance incidents cause undesirable change to a project and can delay a project in a never-ending cascade of lost time. If these incidents are just accepted as par for the course, they can cause 30% to 40% change on a project. They *can,* however, be prevented or minimized and must be managed quickly before they reach such a magnitude.

## Managing Non-compliance Changes

The first line of non-compliance prevention is one of defense. Careful consideration must be given to the likelihood of non-compliance change during the initial definition of a project when the statement of work is being prepared. This is when project risk analysis occurs. Those areas that suggest high risk in the event of non-compliance should be very specifically identified and their potential impact on the project emphasized. If they are identified as items of risk, then probability and consequence can be applied. That means their likelihood of occurrence and the cost or schedule impact can be predicted. By this method their importance is made more visible to everyone, and non-compliance is less likely to occur.

In the event that non-compliance changes do begin to creep into the picture, the most effective approach to dealing with them involves three steps:

1. Provide every team member with an opportunity to record non-compliance occurrences.

   Every team member is given an opportunity to provide project status in narrative form and in quantitative form. On the narrative-based Weekly Progress Report (see exhibit 10), there are sections titled "This week I lost time due to: (specify hours)" and "Problems that may cause me future lost time are:". Every incident of lost time greater than one half hour in the preceding week should be reflected on this report. The project team also considers their activities for the upcoming week and highlights any potential items that might cause lost time.

   The project team also maintains an ongoing *lost time log* (exhibit 12). At any time during the day that they experience lost time because of non-compliance problems, they are expected to record an entry in the lost time log.

**KEANE**

# Lost Time Log

| Date: | Hrs. Lost | Reason: | Resolution: |
|-------|-----------|---------|-------------|
| 4/7 | .5 | LAN # 8 down | |
| 4/20 | 2.0 | Server repairs | |
| 4/21 | 6 | Software install | Schedule for off shift |
| 4/21 | .5 | LAN # 8 down | |
| 4/26 | 1.0 | LAN # 8 down | Meet with tech. services |
| 4/29 | .5 | LAN # 8 down | |
| 5/2 | 4.0 | LAN # 8 down | Escalate to tech. serv. mgt. |

2. Quickly accumulate summary data relevant to the frequency and total effect of non-compliance occurrences.

   The project manager reviews the lost time log daily and reviews the weekly progress reports as they are received. He or she must note any repetitious incidents that may have serious impact on the project. The incidents should be recorded and the cumulative effect summarized in terms of lost hours and dollars.

3. Eradicate non-compliance problems and prevent their future occurrence.

   The project manager now must determine the best method of dealing with the problems. There may be personal issues involved that will require careful one-on-one dealings. At times, it may only be necessary to bring to one person's attention the cumulative but considerable impact that his or her non-compliance problems are having on the overall project. Your management skills will be put to the test in your efforts to prevent non-compliance incidents.

What follows is an example of one project's non-compliance problems and their resolution:

The delivery date for a PC to mainframe server was continually delayed, because the technical services group and customer could not agree on a configuration. The failure to agree increasingly impacted the project as more programs and programmers reached a point when they could not test.

The project manager brought up the problem regarding the server every week at the project status meeting and also separately petitioned the respective managers to resolve the problem quickly. Little progress appeared to be taking place. After week three of the continuing problem, a simple status sheet (exhibit 13) accompanied the weekly project status reports sent to all managers in Information Systems, Customer Services, and Technical Services.

| Exhibit 13: Lost Time Summary | | | | |
|---|---|---|---|---|
| | **Week One** | **Week Two** | **Week Three** | **Week Four** |
| Hours Lost | 12 | 16 | 27 | 45 |
| Project Cost | $480 | $640 | $1,080 | $1,800 |
| Cumulative Costs | $480 | $1,120 | $2,200 | $4,000 |

Note: The completion date of the project has slipped one full week because of the problem.

While this may appear a rather harsh measure for resolving the problem, the project manager and his manager agreed that it would be the quickest and most effective approach. In this case, the server was in place by the fifth week. Who knows how long it might have gone without such action.

As with design change, non-compliance change should be charged to the *change budget.* It is not part of the original estimate, and its impact will be exceedingly clear as less money and fewer hours are available in the change budget for the more important design changes sure to surface later in the project. The prudent project manager will take the necessary steps to prevent non-compliance change and to establish an effective process for managing design changes.

## Chapter Summary: Establish a Change Procedure

1. A formal procedure for managing change should be employed for every project. Without exception, all changes should be subject to that procedure.

2. If change is not formally managed, there is little likelihood that a project will be completed on time and within budget.

3. Keane identifies two types of change. Design change arises when another way of doing things (usually a better way) has been suggested or mandated. Non-compliance change is a failure of someone or something to meet a commitment.

4. In order to recognize and measure change, the project must be baselined.

5. Projects should include a change budget, which is set aside at the beginning of each project. ALL changes are subsequently charged to that change budget.

6. The percentage of change tends to be consistent across projects. Organizations must track this historically to determine what that percentage is.

7. The change budget can be controlled by the customer or some other person who can provide balance of power.

8. Non-compliance changes must be closely tracked, their cumulative effect on the project carefully measured and communicated, and every effort made to eliminate them as quickly as possible.

# 6 Principle Six: Agree on Acceptance Criteria

# Agree on Acceptance Criteria

In the final Principle of Productivity Management, the focus is on having the customer approve deliverable products and, in turn, accepting the completed system. Don't be fooled; delivering a system that the customer accepts is not always easy. Too often, the development team has all but disappeared into a cave to work on the project and emerged with what they think is a perfect product, only to have the customer reject it.

Sometimes there will be strong resistance from customers to accept a new or modified system. Perhaps they genuinely do not want the new system but circumstances are forcing it on them: the introduction of new computer technology or a corporate mandate might require it. Perhaps there is an economic advantage to leaving the system in the hands of Information Systems so they do not have to devote time, money, training, people, space, or other resources to it. Such resistance can delay acceptance and impede progress.

If you have followed the other five principles, however, gaining acceptance should be almost an afterthought. If you have defined the project in detail and have managed an effective team through the completion of deliverable products using the 80-Hour Rule—adjusting for change as necessary— the customer will have been involved all along and will know exactly what to expect from the final product.

There are of course some guidelines to follow to make sure acceptance is clear and contains no surprises for you or for the customer.

## Rules of the Acceptance Game

### Orient the Project Team to Acceptance

Before implementing the mechanics of an acceptance procedure, you and the customer must set some rules that govern acceptance during the project. First, of course, you need to establish with them that there will actually be a formal process of acceptance for the project. The customer may assume that you will deliver a system at the end of the project and that they will simply begin using it. In order to avoid such a misconception, the project manager must orient all parties to the acceptance process before the project starts. You should identify a formal process for reviewing and accepting completed work during the preparation of the statement of work. It is at project initiation that the extended team is united in the project effort and will provide the most enthusiastic support. This is the project manager's best opportunity to set solid rules.

## Acceptance as a Gradual Process

The second rule is that all parties should regard acceptance as a gradual process occurring throughout the project rather than as a onetime event at the end of the project. Overall acceptance will be tied directly to the acceptance of each short-term deliverable product being approved over the life of the project. That is not to say that, just because a product is accepted, it cannot change. The process of change will continue to occur over the life of the project. Formal acceptance procedures do, however, help to prevent unnecessary change.

If acceptance is gained gradually throughout system development as the components of the system are completed, the task becomes much less forbidding both to customers and developers. The customers make a "creeping commitment" as they gain vested ownership of the system, and the developers have the satisfaction of regular accomplishments. A series of small, controlled acceptances should accumulate, leading gradually to total acceptance. When you reach the end, you need be concerned only with acceptance of the few remaining items.

## Products Are Real

The third rule is that products delivered throughout the project are real components of the overall system. The customer should realize that these interim deliverables are parts of the final product, not prototypes. Unless a formal change is approved later, the customer is approving a product for use in the final system when they accept a deliverable.

## Acceptance Criteria

The final and most important rule is that you must establish—*in advance*—a set of criteria with which to judge whether something is accepted or rejected. What are the criteria of each deliverable product? Each major milestone? Each phase? The entire system? Acceptance criteria are the guidelines for the development team to design the correct system functions and for the customer to determine whether the system is what they asked for. Establishing acceptance criteria is part of the planning and design phases and should happen no later. It is crucial that you agree on these criteria before starting any work on the project; otherwise, you would be starting the project before you knew how to end it.

*Mutual understanding of the final product should be established at the start of the project.*

Below is one set of the more broad acceptance criteria for the data collection portion of a laboratory reporting system developed for a pharmaceutical company. The system collects pharmaceutical test results from sites around the world. Based on the following criteria, the design team was able to clearly define and track tasks, and the customer knew exactly how to evaluate the finished product:

- The program will be capable of polling at least 12 collection sites every 30 minutes.

- All data will be collected via satellite communication links.

- The system must be capable of transmitting at 28,800 bps.

- The system will compile a transaction logging report.

Acceptance criteria will vary significantly depending on the technical nature of the product, size of the product or milestone, and its position within the development life cycle. In some instances the criteria will focus on technical issues as above, and in others the criteria may be more concerned with meeting certain business needs.

The acceptance criteria will also serve as the basis for rejection when it occurs. For the customer to say, "This is just wrong!" is an inadequate rejection. The customers must describe as best they can everything that makes the product "wrong," thus providing a *rejection with cause.* If the customer rejects a product, you want to get as many specific problems on the table as possible so you can correct them all during system revision. If the reasons for rejection do not correspond to the established acceptance criteria, you will probably need to redefine those criteria.

# Actual Acceptance

## The Formal Acceptance Process

The acceptance process needs to be "formal" only to the extent that everyone will be able to follow it. Only if the process is well defined will you avoid misunderstandings and ensure measured progress.

The essential elements of any acceptance procedure are

1. Identify with the customer which key products and milestones acceptance will depend upon. These are generally tangible, less technical items that represent the system to the customer such as monitor screen layouts, maps and panels for data entry or reporting, hard copy reports, forms, procedures, file or record layouts to confirm data being retained, and test results. These products should be identified in the work breakdown structure.

2. Identify an individual or individuals from the customer organization who have the authority and ability to accept or reject with cause. In order for the acceptance process to work effectively, there must be customer representatives who fully understand that if they sign off on all deliverables, the system will be accepted.

   Occasionally, different customers will be responsible for different levels of deliverables. A person with administrative functions in accounts payable may be the right person to sign off on a single reconciliation report but not to sign off on the entire new accounts payable system. Under these circumstances, it is essential that the person with the authority to accept the entire system be identified from the beginning and that he or she be involved at some mid-project milestones. It is the project manager's responsibility to make sure that the right people are involved approving products along the way. If you hear statements like "It looks okay but we won't really know until my boss takes a look at it," then the boss should be the one responsible for acceptance.

3. Establish a turnaround time for acceptance or rejection with cause. (It is best to work in terms of business days.) Generally, if written acceptance or rejection is not received within the allotted time frame, the items in question are assumed complete and accepted for use in the system. This "acceptance through default," however, should be avoided, since it creates the potential for misunderstanding and customer dissatisfaction.

4. Prepare a written acceptance/rejection form (exhibit 14) that indicates the date, item(s) being submitted for acceptance, perhaps their value in hours or dollars, and who is submitting them. Provide a space for the customer to sign the document and a space to note the reasons for rejection.

These acceptance procedures should be defined in the statement of work and should be exercised as early in the project as possible. By following the rules from day one, you ensure that everyone knows those rules from the start.

## The System Test Plan

In the stages before you can show the system actually working, the best way to demonstrate how it will work is with the plans of how to test the system. The *system test plan* describes those tests that demonstrate how the system functions; it is the most important acceptance document. The system test plan is completed during the analysis and design phases.

Preparation of system test plans should be viewed as an iterative and evolutionary process. A test plan generally cannot be completed in one sitting, because as more detail is developed during the design phases, it is refined and updated to reflect changes. The test plans must be complete before any actual programming or construction is started. The project team's ability to prepare a system test plan is an excellent

# K
**KEANE**

# Product/Task Acceptance

Client Name: _____Bristol_____    Client No.: _____

Project Name: _____BEPS_____    Project No.: _____

Prod./Task Name: _Sales Commissions_    Prod./Task No. _____

**Description:**

1. Sales commissions on-line

2. Sales commissions monthly summary report

**Keane Acceptance:**

■ Approve    ☐ Disapprove

Signature: _B. Wyatt - Project Manager_    Date: _6/17_

**Client Acceptance:**

☐ Approve    ☐ Disapprove

Signature: _____    Date: _____

Remarks:

indication that the team fully understands the system requirements and acceptance criteria. It helps serve as a check on whether the design is complete enough to proceed to the construction phases of development. Simply preparing the system test plan will often point out where the design requires more attention.

The system test plan should define in detail precisely what constitutes an acceptable system by describing specific tests that are objective and measurable. This is one area that should not be left to subjective or independent judgment. The entire extended team should be involved in the preparation of test plans. Disagreements during final systems testing can become bitter.

Since the system test plan is the culmination of the design effort and a critical component of final acceptance, the customer's active participation in preparing it is essential. This participation is ensured if the system test team includes at least one customer representative. The project team is qualified to know what will constitute technical readiness, but the customer—who will have to live with the system—is more qualified to know what the system should actually be doing. In the event that the customer does not feel qualified to know what they want, Information Systems has a responsibility to convey the necessary knowledge. Qualified or not, the customer must assume the responsibility for accepting or rejecting the results of these tests.

A formal review of the system test plan by the customer is essential to ensure that as many design errors and omissions as possible are detected before coding begins. A review of the test plan provides the customer with a comprehensive overview of the entire system. It also identifies the quantity and skill level of resources the customers must have available for final testing of the system. It is not unusual for the final customer testing, as defined in the system test plan, to require individuals from several different segments of the customer's business. The system test plan will help put them on notice that when the day of reckoning comes, they had better be prepared to provide the resources in the quantity required and for the time periods needed.

Make sure everyone from all customer and user departments agrees to the test plans before actual construction begins. From a very broad perspective these plans should ensure that all the "business needs" have been met. A system test plan should demonstrate that the system (1) will address the problem, need, or opportunity; (2) will meet all specifications and expectations; (3) will actually be usable by the customers; and (4) will efficiently provide adequate payback.

Just before system testing begins, the system test plan is reviewed one last time to (1) ensure that any changes made during coding are incorporated, (2) reestablish the commitment of all concerned parties, and (3) reaffirm that, if its specifications are met, the system is acceptable.

## System Testing

The true measure of the system's functions is in the actual testing. After the completion of a deliverable, the project manager arranges a system test to walk the customer through the product. When all testing indicated in the test plan is satisfactorily completed, the project itself is complete and the system belongs to the customer.

The amount of time spent in testing over the life of a project is considerable. Software and systems development testing can vary considerably. If your organization is developing software for guided missiles, a space shot, or some other mission-critical system that involves human lives, the percentage of time spent testing may be as high as 90%. Other software developers will certainly spend a smaller percentage of time on it. For most projects, 25% to 30% of the entire time budget will be devoted to testing functions. This includes all forms of testing such as design and spec walk-throughs, unit tests, regression tests, system tests, integration tests, stress tests, etc.

Testing is crucial to the overall success of any project and consequently is not the place to cut corners. This includes planning for tests as well as actually performing the tests. It would not be unusual to spend as much time planning tests as is actually spent in performing the tests.

## Acceptance of Technical Products Within the Development Team

When discussing acceptance, we tend to focus on the customer judging the work of the development team. Larger projects, however, often benefit from formal acceptance procedures within the development team. It is unlikely that customers will be qualified to approve and accept technical products such as program unit test plans, database schemas, and fourth level data flow diagrams, nor are they likely to want to—qualified or not. But these technical items should be formally accepted just as items that are delivered to the customers. The project manager may want to establish an additional acceptance process involving only the development team for these technical products. The process is exactly the same as the one with the customer.

For acceptance of technical products within the development team, a hierarchy of acceptance is established within the chain of command on the project: Developers take products to senior programmers or lead analysts for approval. In turn, the senior programmers or lead analysts may take comprehensive products to the project leader or project manager for acceptance. Project leaders and project managers then submit items to the customers. The individual(s) who will participate in the acceptances of the more technical products should be identified in advance in the statement of work.

## Review Acceptance Criteria at the End of Each Phase

The acceptance process should be reviewed at the end of each phase and specifically defined (or redefined) for the following phase. The person(s) responsible for acceptance and what they accept can change throughout the life of the project. The products of each phase vary considerably. In the System Concept Phase, for example, we are dealing principally with narratives and business-oriented documentation. In the Construction Phase, the key products are unit test plans, computer programs, and unit test results. This variation is one of the reasons that, at Keane, we place such emphasis on revising the statement of work at the end of each phase. It continually reinforces that we are doing the right thing at the right time and for the overall right purpose.

## Measuring System Performance

A system may be working, but is it working well enough? Some sort of performance and quality measurements are necessary as part of the acceptance process. What they are, however, should be determined individually based on the project.

A simplified example of performance measurement acceptance testing is reflected in the comparisons between the following two new systems. At the conclusion of system testing, System A and System B were running perfectly. But System A had suffered a defect rate of 28.6 errors per 100,000 lines of code and System B's defect rate was 2.4 per 100,000 lines of code. A simple extrapolation based on this company's history suggests not only that System A will fail more frequently in the ensuing years of usage, but that the maintenance cost will approach $730,000 compared to less than $55,000 for System B. Under such circumstances, System A may be deemed unacceptable even though it is now working fine.

In the past we, as an industry, have been reluctant to deal with the issue of performance measurement. It is now being thrust upon us by the demands of more effective performance and international competition. Many of the organizations that Keane deals with are hesitantly poking at it. It is our opinion that by the turn of the century much of what we do may have some performance measurements associated with the acceptance process.

# The Impact of New Development Techniques on Acceptance

Project management and the systems development process are being continually changed by advances in computer technology. This is true of nearly every aspect of our lives. In order to benefit from new multimedia, for example, we must learn to operate new devices and deal with more complex procedures.

The first cars that rolled off Mr. Ford's assembly line did not take long for the customer to test for acceptance. There were not that many complicated features: essentially, a motor, three pedals—forward, reverse, stop—and a throttle lever for speed. A few other gizmos helped.

Today's automobiles have an growing array of features that go beyond meeting simple transportation needs. The careful customer must be knowledgeable over a much broader technical base. This is also true of today's computer systems. There is much more technology involved that must be tested and approved by the purchasing customer.

It was not long ago that the customer's business requirements were described in simple, narrative documents written in common business terms. Now, many organizations utilize structured analysis techniques and various CASE tools to help define their business requirements. These techniques are composed of written procedures and automated software that run on PCs and large, mainframe computers. The output from these applications may consist of charts, diagrams, data models, and documents written in various forms of structured language. Customers may have to become familiar with some of these complex technical outputs in order to actively participate in the acceptance process.

Organizations frequently have a large selection of development aids available to them. Each new project presents an opportunity to select the aids that will provide the most effective development. That means there could be wide variety of the products that may be identified for formal acceptance. Each product should be reviewed and identified at the beginning of each project, and the customers and extended team members must become familiar with them.

## Chapter Summary: Agree on Acceptance Criteria

1. All projects must possess a formal process for the acceptance or rejection with cause of deliverable products.

2. The acceptance/rejection process must be defined and included as a segment of the Statement of Work.

3. Everyone on the project team must understand and agree to the process of formal acceptance.

4. Acceptance should be viewed as a series of small acceptances rather than as one large occurrence at the end of the project or phase.

5. The criteria for which acceptance will be judged must be determined at the beginning of the project.

6. Never begin a job unless you know what it will look like at the end.

7. The individual(s) responsible for acceptance must be identified at the beginning of the project. They must be aware that, as they accept each deliverable, they are accepting the product for final use in the system.

8. A written document should accompany all items submitted for acceptance.

9. The system test plan is an evolving document that is begun during requirements definition and is refined during the Business Systems Analysis and Technical Design phases.

10. Acceptance can be viewed as a hierarchical process that goes from the most junior developer to the highest level customer.

11. The changing nature of automated processes continually creates new products for acceptance. The project manager and team must review the impact of these new deliverable products for each project.

# 7 Conclusion

# Conclusion

## Completing a Project

Projects have an amazing capacity for achieving the status of "almost finished." We previously mentioned a couple of reasons for this from both the customer and Information Systems perspectives. Whether the resistance is coming from the customer or from the development team, the project manager must doggedly pursue the goal of the customer taking over the project. If implemented properly, the six Principles of Productivity Management will guide you swiftly toward that goal.

### Project Completion Meetings

As soon as you can see some light at the end of the tunnel on a project, start scheduling *project completion meetings*. The very name alerts the project team that the job is coming to an end. The psychological impact of attending something called a "project completion meeting" is probably more powerful than what might take place at the meeting.

The meetings should focus on the few remaining tasks to be completed in order to gain final acceptance for the project. Each team member should compile a list of project completion tasks. It is an opportunity for the team to regroup and remind themselves of the project's goals and how close they are to being achieved. With continual encouragement and enthusiasm from the project manager at the last stages of the project—and of course with the work of the development team—the final tasks and testing will get done.

### Schedule All Final Testing

Make sure all final testing is scheduled. The project will never be complete if adequate testing has not been successfully concluded. If test data must be prepared for these tests, assign that task appropriately. Set up dates, schedule the necessary computer time, put operations on notice, line up communication channels … whatever it takes. Be certain to consider all the appropriate testing for your project: Unit, Stress, Integration, System, Customer Acceptance, Regression, etc. This is probably a good time to also begin reviewing any configuration management concerns.

## Involve All Production Turnover Groups

Completing a project suggests that it will actually become a production system. This means that the system moves from a development responsibility to a production responsibility. This transition is a good item to review with the entire team at a project team meeting. You might even have someone from production support come in and explain the process. This will add a sense of import and urgency. Make sure all library and database dispositions are reviewed.

## Plan Resource Distribution

You should by now have in hand a Gantt chart or some form of project plan that clearly reflects the decrease in responsibility of the project team. It should show very clearly when an individual's work is completed and that he or she will no longer be charged to the project. All management parties need to know of the new availability as soon as possible. It is your responsibility to make sure that management fully understands that the team is done after the specified date.

If you do not assume this responsibility, you may find yourself keeping someone on a project because there is simply no place for them to go at the moment. Such situations chew up project hours and dollars and do not reflect work performed. If continued, this scenario can soon turn a successful project into one that shows an overrun when the final numbers are counted. And it is the final numbers that people will remember.

## Prepare Project Team Evaluations

As a project manager, you must assume some responsibility for reporting on the performance of your team. This is the case even if you have people on the team who do not report directly to you. Whether you are required to complete a formal performance report or you are simply asked for casual observations by the person's manager in the hallway, you should be prepared to give an informed, honest answer.

Give yourself an ample amount of time with the project reports in order to consider the performance of each individual on the project team. Try to make clear observations and draw objective conclusions. If you do not take the time to record your thoughts when they are fresh in your mind, they will fade quickly, and you will be of little help to the team members and their managers. Later, the opinion will be much more subjective, will certainly lack details, and may even be incorrect.

## Prepare Financial Summaries

This is the time to pull together all the final reporting … especially relating to financial issues. You have run a good project, and it is time to make sure your performance will be immortalized. If there have been problems and cost overruns, it is especially important to collect and review the financials. We have admonished ourselves and the industry over and over for not measuring and accurately reporting what we do. Once again, we will never get better unless we can begin measuring. If we do not accurately reflect costs to the project now, how will we know to do it better next time?

## Project Reviews

One of the greatest contributions you can now make to yourself and to your organization is to conduct a review of the completed project. This is often inaccurately referred to as a project "postmortem." A postmortem is an examination after death that would be appropriate if we were examining a failed or canceled project, but for a successful one, it should be called a "project review" or "project audit." And all projects should get one.

The project review will provide the most effective way to improve project management practices. Individuals and organizations can effect a three- to fivefold increase in performance through lessons learned from the project review process.

The project review, like the project itself, should involve all of the key extended team members: customers, Information Systems, operations, technical services, managers, vendors, etc. It should be conducted as soon as possible after the completion of the project—no more than 30 days later. The review should be formal, should have an assigned note-taker and a facilitator in charge, and should take place in a meeting room with ample facilities. Typically, the project manager will act as the facilitator, but this does not have to be the case. The project manager is responsible for making all arrangements, ensuring that all the right people are present and that all necessary materials and documentation are available.

This review must answer two questions: "What did we do right?" and "What could we have done better?" This will help keep the project review focused on the issues important to your organization. In a later review session, you (the project manager) and your manager may want to have a similar discussion about the most important skills necessary to be successful in your organization. This will give you an opportunity to evaluate your performance and gain insight into areas of improvement for your next project.

The project review team should begin by drafting a list of the eight or ten items considered most important for a successful project. Because of the changing nature of organizations, this list should be redrafted for each project. The elements of success will vary considerably among projects. A typical list may look like the following:

- Customer expectations met

- All specifications achieved

- Project completed on time

- Project completed within budget

- ROI/IRR achieved

- Project met organizational goals and strategies

- Project provided good experience for project team

In addition, a list of the eight or ten major problems encountered during the project should be compiled. Do not let these lists become directed toward individual performance; keep them process oriented. Keep these two lists conspicuously posted somewhere in the room, and use them to keep discussion focused.

Although there may be overlap between the lists and even within one list, their development will provide an effective beginning for a successful project review.

You will find that the information derived from these lists will fall into two broad categories: objective and subjective. The objective will largely deal with dates, dollars, and hours and will reflect measures of team productivity, costs per deliverable products, and defects measurements. The remainder will deal with individual opinions and perceptions. Both are important to capture accurately.

When the project review is completed it is important that the results be communicated appropriately throughout the organization. This too is the project manager's responsibility, probably in conjunction with his or her manager. The appropriate narrative documents, charts and graphs, reports, etc., should be neatly presented and well packaged for readability.

When the project review task is completed, the project is done and the project manager's responsibilities for the project are complete. This is the last task to be charged to the project, and the customer and the project manager's manager should sign off on it.

# Fostering Project Management Practices Within Organizations

The successful implementation of project management practices within an organization not accustomed to them can often be a long and frustrating experience. It usually involves considerable cultural and procedural change. This change cannot be simply mandated by even the most ranking individual within the organization. Neither will putting the entire population through project management training programs guarantee the use of project management procedures. In order for the process to succeed, it must also be demonstrated to have practical and economic worth, and there must be support groups and processes in place. Years of maintaining project management principles at Keane and assisting other companies to implement those principles have taught us that the right approach is crucial.

The following steps for introducing project management are presented in approximate chronological order. Taking these steps will provide initial exposure to project management practices. More than anything else, however, recognizing the benefits gained from using project management will ultimately provide the most effective impetus for its further use and success. This will occur only as a result of using project management procedures on real projects.

## Develop an Organizationally Appropriate SDLC

If it has not yet been done, the organization should focus on developing the appropriate systems development life cycles. There should be a unique SDLC for each approach used in your organization. That is: Traditional Waterfall, Rapid

Iterative Development, Prototype, Package Purchase, Client-Server, etc. Ideally, the life cycles should be available in printed binder form and on some computer-accessible medium that is available to mainframe and PC users.

The conceptual understanding and consequent use of the systems development life cycle is not as easily mastered as might be assumed. We have found that additional classroom training is required in order for practitioners to competently use an SDLC to create a project work breakdown structure. This material can usually be covered in a day-and-a-half to two-day program. It is most effective if preceded by an introductory project management program or included as part of a three-day project management training program.

## Prepare Project Management Guidebook

Many organizations benefit from having a guidebook for using good project management practices. The guidebook is a set of documents that helps define the how-to's of project management. It covers all major areas such as preparation of the statement of work, report preparation, use of software, forms to use, setting up testing procedures, using an SDLC, and virtually anything else associated with the project management activity. A Project Management Review Team can be instrumental in helping set up this guidebook. The following brief outline is typical of one for a small organization:

- Introduction
- Overview of Project Management - Definitions
- Systems Development Life Cycles (Development Approaches)
- Planning a Project
    - Identifying Requirements
    - Statement of Work
    - Estimating

- Risk Assessment and Mitigation

- Project Plans

- Automated Tools

- Planning for Quality Assurance

■ Managing a Project

- Progress Tracking and Status Reporting

- Change Control

- Acceptance of Deliverable Products

- Testing

■ Project Completion

## Project Management Review Teams

The establishment of a small, internal organization that will help support project management techniques and procedures can significantly enhance the incorporation of project management within the organization. Keane's approach is to have an individual identified as the *project officer* at each of its branches. Other organizations have established similar positions that support large business units or have identified a specific team of three to six individuals who support the entire organization.

The principal function of these individuals is to mentor other project managers and project leaders. They assist in defining projects, preparing statements of work, estimating and validating project costs and schedules, assigning and leveling resources, tracking projects and reporting progress, and providing counsel on the difficult task of managing a project. They also help establish procedures, select software, review projects, train project management, provide public relations support, and perform any other activities associated with project management.

## Project Management Training

Project management has now become a well-recognized discipline. There are right ways to do it, and they can be defined. If you manage projects the right way, they get done more rapidly, at less cost, with a high level of customer satisfaction, and with fewer project team members biting the dust. The specifics of acceptable project management can be taught. Consequently, increasing numbers of organizations now require that their project managers be correctly trained in all project management phases.

Many organizations even require that project managers be certified. This means that they have attended the appropriate training sessions and have passed the series of examinations required for certification.

Any individual can achieve project management certification whether the company has mandated it or not. Many colleges and universities offer curricula through their continuing education programs that lead to project management certification. There is an international organization called the Project Management Institute,* which offers a highly regarded level of certification. There are other private training organizations that also provide excellent project management training.

As an example, the Project Management Institute requires qualifications in four main areas:

- Experience
- Education
- Service to the project management industry
- Completion of an evaluative exam

The evaluative exam consists of 320 questions in six parts. It is taken in a seven-hour sitting and comprises the following broad categories:

* Project Management Institute, 130 South State Road, Upper Darby, PA 19082. (610) 734-3330

- Scope Management

- Quality Management

- Time Management

- Cost Management

- Risk Management

- Human Resources Management

- Contract/Procurement Management

- Communications Management

## Selling Project Management in the Organization

One would think that a process as obviously beneficial as project management would be readily accepted in any organization. It can, however, represent a significant departure from existing procedures, and such change is frequently resisted. In addition to the previously noted steps, it may be necessary to mount a public relations and training campaign. The steps noted below represent a series of events and activities that represent Keane's most effective process for helping an organization assimilate to project management.

One successful approach is to identify a high-ranking corporate sponsor. We have frequently found such sponsors in various management positions within the Information Systems departments. In that case it doesn't have to be the ranking manager, director, VP, or CIO. Generally speaking though, the higher the seniority, the better. We have also found very successful sponsors or advocates within the various IS customer organizations and within training departments.

Another PR approach we have found effective is to put on an hour-long program on project management and invite some potential ranking supporters. This can be billed in any form you think would be attractive to your organization. Examples might be "Effective Project Management and Increased Profits," "How to Run More Successful Projects," "Project Management State-of-the-Art," etc. This might be scheduled as a breakfast session or perhaps a brown-bag lunch seminar. Even if you have to bring someone from outside the organization to assist or to make the presentation, you will find it worthwhile. Use the opportunity to feel out the group and identify some potential sponsors.

Viewed as a sequence of events, this is the appropriate time to present an executive-level seminar. This might be a three- to six-hour program presented to high-level IS personnel and customers. Keep this at 10 to 15 people, and arrange them in a U-shaped room so there will be ample opportunity for cross-discussion and questions. Keep this session informative and rapidly moving. Make sure you have plenty of handouts that describe what you are trying to do within the organization and why it is to their benefit.

Once this level of interest has been stimulated within an organization, a small group should attend a formal project management seminar of two to three days. The location of the seminar will depend on the size of the organization. If it is large enough, Keane will conduct one of our in-house project management seminars for 15 to 20 people. With a smaller organization, we will encourage them to send some people to a public seminar. This initial exposure to the seminars informs them of the project management process and training techniques, and it allows them to evaluate the effectiveness of such a training program for their organization. Individuals who have attended these seminars usually become very supportive of the organization moving to good project management practices.

In any of these sessions, try to get the Information Systems people and their customers in attendance. You will also find it beneficial to have each program kicked off and/or concluded by a high-level organizational sponsor. This can make a big difference in how well received the entire process is.

As soon as possible, run and closely monitor a small project using all the project management principles and techniques. You will be able to identify many benefits and advantages. Widely publicize these successes. It is the live demonstration of project management success that will provide the ultimate assurance of its continued implementation within an organization.

## Play the Game, Don't Just Watch It

Project management is not a vicarious sport. It is not meant to be watched from afar like a Sunday football game. It is meant to be played on the active field of the organizational business. It is the doing of project management that will allow the organization to reap the many rewards it has to offer. While there is certainly training that needs to be provided, procedures to be developed, and software to be learned, do not allow your organization to become so involved in these activities that you forget to play the game. Success will come with experience. Experience comes only with active participation.

Project management is now one of the most widely practiced forms of management in the U.S. and other Western countries. Our experience suggests that it is not quite as popular in the East, but there is certainly a growing level of awareness and interest in the Pacific Rim countries. We believe project management will continue to grow in popularity for a simple reason: it provides the singularly most effective technique for managing resources toward a specific purpose and within a calendar schedule. With that in mind, Keane will continue to focus significant development, training, finances, and resources toward the successful management of projects.

## Experience Starts Here

Although we have made our very best attempt to provide you with the benefits of our project management experience, we certainly have not been all-inclusive. That simply cannot be done in any written form—no matter the weight of the tome. There must also be some look, feel, and touch. We leave you then with the encouragement to seek added dimensions elsewhere. Read other books that offer different perspectives, enroll in seminars, join organizations, subscribe to publications, and attend your local college and university extension classes.

Project management presents a very rewarding career opportunity that is at a threshold of need. But the serious contenders for these opportunities will have to possess some genuine credentials; they will actually have to know something about what they are doing. Project management is no longer a loosely defined exercise of subjective probables. It is measurable, learnable, and fairly straightforward to implement.

Project management is only rewarding and beneficial, however, to the extent that it is actually used. Organizations cannot become more effective until projects are better managed. In order to make better use of people, to meet increasingly tighter deadlines, and to ensure that we stay within budget and profit guidelines, we must actually use the proven techniques. We suggest you start using them today and build the experience in order to become successful in this role. Use project management techniques, track the successes and the problems so you will be better at it next time, and the next and the next.

We invite you to join with us in a practice that has the potential to considerably improve information technology and the software development and maintenance world. It is as exciting now as it was 30 years ago. Our bet is that it will be equally as exciting and enticing for the next 30. Successful project management will continue to be an integral—and increasingly more important—part of that excitement.

## Project Management Checklist

The checklist in exhibit 15 serves as a final review of the main points covered by the Principles of Productivity Management.

### Exhibit 15: Project Management Checklist

#### Initial Project Review

1. Begin the preparation of the statement of work.
2. Meet with the customers and information processing management to review their objectives and responsibilities.
3. Produce a project organization chart to identify the key individuals and their positions relative to the project.
4. Determine staff availability.
5. Review budgets, objectives, and milestones.
6. Review schedules.
7. Review standards and methodologies.
8. Review any project control/accounting reporting procedures and systems.
9. Decide on a development approach.
10. Clearly define all products. Prepare a document identifying all customer-significant, deliverable products.

#### Preliminary Planning

11. Break the job down into manageable tasks. Create the work breakdown structure.
12. Determine assignments by skill level.
13. Develop time estimates with team members.
14. Determine and finalize individual schedules; assign in writing individual team members to each task.
15. Enter all data into the project management software.
16. Define the change procedures.
17. Define the acceptance criteria and procedures.
18. Finalize all budgets.
19. Prepare a project plan with a software package or according to organization guidelines.
20. Prepare a schedule of deliverable products.
21. Prepare a deliverable-versus-budget schedule indicating the

**Exhibit 15 (continued)**

hours or dollars to be expended by week versus the number of products delivered by week.

22. Prepare a formal time and cost estimate, identifying the major tasks, hours, and dollars estimated.

23. Validate estimates with a distribution model.

24. Formalize all individual team member assignments and responsibilities.

## Project Confirmation

25. Break the job into acceptable short intervals (80 hours or less). Produce a task list in which all tasks are no longer than 80 hours or two calendar weeks.

26. Formalize change procedure; confirm in writing how changes will be handled for the project.

27. Formalize acceptance criteria; confirm in writing how acceptance will occur for the project.

28. Prepare a Project Control Book.

29. Orient team members in a team meeting.

30. Develop management report formats and project reporting framework. Identify the specific weekly or monthly reports that will be prepared and distributed for the project.

## Tracking

31. Determine task dependencies and critical paths.

32. Prepare weekly timesheets for all team members to report against.

33. Take appropriate steps to maintain team morale and focus.

34. Track all progress against the plan by weekly reporting of hours and dollars.

35. Occasionally track projects through some form of trend analysis.

36. Begin the project completion process.

37. Complete all testing.

38. Turn completed project over to users.

# Chapter Summary: Conclusion

1.  All projects should go through a series of steps as a part of the formal processes of completion. These processes must be identified at the beginning of the project and noted in the statement of work.

2.  The project manager must constantly reinforce the notion that the project will be in the hands of the customer when completed.

3.  Schedule formal project completion meetings for both effect and purpose.

4.  Project completion requires the identification, scheduling, and completion of all testing.

5.  Resources must be scheduled to leave the project as soon as their tasks are completed.

6.  The project manager should prepare evaluations for all project team members.

7.  All project financials must be brought up-to-date and the information summarized.

8.  A formal project review with all team members present should be scheduled within 30 days of project completion.

9.  The use of project management must be fostered throughout the organization through many different approaches.

10. There should be several different systems development life cycles available.

11. Project management practices are greatly augmented by the use of a Project Management Guidebook.

12. The formation of a Project Management Review Team to help mentor project managers is a great benefit to an organization.

13. There are many specialized areas, forms, and depths of project management training available.

14. Project management must frequently be sold to an organization by pointing out the features, advantages, and benefits.

15. No amount of training will take the place of the experience gained by hands-on project management.

# Bibliography

*A Guide to the Project Management Body of Knowledge (PMBOK).*
August 1994. Drexell Hill, PA: Project Management Institute.

Albrecht, Allen J. 1981. "Function Points as a Measure of
Productivity." Presented at GUIDE #53, 12 November, in
Dallas, TX.

Beizer, Boris. 1984. *Software System Testing and Quality Assurance.*
New York, NY: Van Nostrand Reinhold.

Block, Peter. 1991. *The Empowered Manager: Positive Political
Skills at Work.* San Francisco, CA: Jossey-Bass, Inc.

Boehm, Barry W. 1981. *Software Engineering Economics.*
Englewood Cliffs, NJ: Prentice-Hall, Inc.

Boyatzis, Richard E. 1982. *The Competent Manager: A Model for
Effective Performance.* New York, NY: John Wiley & Sons, Inc.

Brooks, Fredrick P., Jr. 1975. *The Mythical Man-Month.* Menlo Park,
CA: Addison-Wesley Publishing Company, Inc.; reprinted 1982.

*Capability Maturity Model.* 1992 Carnegie Mellon University,
Pittsburgh, PA: Software Engineering Institute.

Cohen, Allan R. and Bradford, David L. 1991. *Influence Without
Authority.* New York, NY: John Wiley & Sons, Inc.

Davis, Jack M. 1989. "Planning and Estimating Software." Case
Outlook 89, No. 2.

DeMarco, Tom. 1982. *Controlling Software Projects.* New York, NY:
Yourdon, Inc.

Dreger, Brian J. 1989. *Function Point Analysis.* Englewood Cliffs,
NJ: Prentice-Hall Advanced Reference Series.

Dreger, Brian J. 1992. *Project Management: Effective Scheduling.*
New York, NY: Van Nostrand Reinhold.

Drucker, Peter F. 1974. *Management: Tasks, Responsibilities,
Practices.* New York, NY: Harper & Row.

Edwards, Perry. 1993. *Systems Analysis and Design.* Watsonville,
CA: McGraw-Hill.

Fisher, Roger and Ury, William. 1986. *Getting to Yes: Negotiating
Agreement Without Giving In.* New York, NY: Penguin Books.

Frame, J. Davidson. 1987. *Managing Projects in Organizations.* San
Francisco, CA: Jossey-Bass, Inc.

Gane, Chris. 1989. *Rapid Systems Development.* Englewood Cliffs,
NJ: Prentice-Hall, Inc.

Gause, Donald C. and Weinberg, Gerald M. 1989. *Exploring
Requirements: Quality Before Design.* New York, NY: Dorset
House Publishing.

Glass, Robert L. 1992. *Building Quality Software*. Englewood Cliffs, NJ: Prentice-Hall, Inc.

Graham, Robert J. 1989. *Project Management as if People Mattered*. Bala Cynwyd, Pennsylvania: Primavera Press.

Hamburger, David 1990. *The Project Manager: Risk Taker and Contingency Planner*. Drexell Hill, PA: Project Management Institute, Project Management Journal. Also from a speech on the same topic to Boston PMI Chapter, March 1992.

Hetzel, Bill. 1993. *Making Software Measurement Work*. Wellesley, MA: QED Publishing Group.

Humphrey, Watts S. 1988. "Characterizing the Software Process: A Maturity Process." IEEE Software Magazine 5, (March): 73-79.

Humphrey, Watts S. 1989. *Managing the Software Process*. Menlo Park, CA: Addison-Wesley Publishing Company, Inc.

Kapur, Gobal K. 1991. *Estimating MIS Projects*. San Ramon, CA: Kapur and Associates, Inc., 1984; reprinted ed. San Ramon, CA: Center for Project Management.

Keane, John F., Marilyn Keane, and Mark Teagan. 1984. *Productivity Management in the Development of Computer Applications*. Englewood Cliffs, NJ: Prentice-Hall, Inc.

Kerzner, Harold, Ph.D. 1984. *Project Management: A Systems Approach to Planning, Scheduling and Controlling*. New York, NY: Van Nostrand Reinhold.

Knutson, Joan, and Ira Bitz. 1991. *Project Management: How to Plan and Manage Successful Projects*. New York, NY: AMACOM, American Management Association.

Martin, James. 1989. *Information Engineering*. A Trilogy, Books I, II and III. Englewood Cliffs, NJ: Prentice-Hall, Inc.

Meredith, Jack R., and Samuel J. Mantel Jr. 1985. *Project Management*. New York, NY: John Wiley & Sons, Inc.

Perry, William E. 1991. *Quality Assurance for Information Systems*. Wellesley, MA: QED Information Sciences, Inc.

*Project Management Body of Knowledge (PMBOK)*. 1987. Drexell Hill, PA: Project Management Institute.

*Risk Management: Concepts and Guidance*. 1986. Ft. Belvoir, VA: Defense Systems Management College

Rowe, William D. 1977. *An Anatomy of Risk*. New York, NY: John Wiley & Sons, Inc.

Schulmeyer, G. Gordon, and James I. McManus. 1992. *Handbook of Software Quality Assurance. 2nd ed.* New York, NY: Van Nostrand Reinhold.

Tenner, Arthur R., and Irving J. DeToro. 1992. *Total Quality Management.* Reading, MA: Addison-Wesley Publishing Company, Inc.

Yourdon, Edward. 1989. *Modern Structured Analysis.* Englewood Cliffs, NJ: Prentice-Hall, Inc.

Yourdon, Edward. 1992. *Decline & Fall of the American Programmer.* Englewood Cliffs, NJ: Yourdon Press.

# Index